DO IT YOURSELF

Manchester University Press

DO IT YOURSELF
MAKING POLITICAL THEATRE

COMMON/WEALTH

Evie Manning and Rhiannon White, with Jenny Hughes

MANCHESTER UNIVERSITY PRESS

Copyright © Evie Manning, Rhiannon White and Jenny Hughes 2025

The right of Evie Manning, Rhiannon White and Jenny Hughes to be identified as the authors of this work has been asserted in accordance with the Copyright, Designs and Patents Act 1988.

Every effort has been made to trace all copyright holders of the material in this book to gain permission for reproduction. Anyone with further copyright information is invited to contact Common/Wealth.

Published by Manchester University Press
Oxford Road, Manchester, M13 9PL

www.manchesteruniversitypress.co.uk

British Library Cataloguing-in-Publication Data
A catalogue record for this book is available from the British Library

ISBN 978 1 5261 9297 4 paperback

First published 2025

The publisher has no responsibility for the persistence or accuracy of URLs for any external or third-party internet websites referred to in this book, and does not guarantee that any content on such websites is, or will remain, accurate or appropriate.

EU authorised representative for GPSR:
Easy Access System Europe, Mustamäe tee 50, 10621 Tallinn, Estonia
gpsr.requests@easproject.com

Typeset
by Cheshire Typesetting Ltd, Cuddington, Cheshire

# CONTENTS

LIST OF CONTRIBUTORS .................................................................................... viii
FOREWORD ............................................................................................................. x
WHY WE WROTE THIS BOOK ............................................................................. xiv

**COMMON/WEALTH MANIFESTO** ...................................................................... 1

## IN COMMON

**What is Common/Wealth?** ................................................................................. 4
What is common? ................................................................................................... 6
What is common is wealth ................................................................................... 7
Being common ........................................................................................................ 9
Where Common/Wealth comes from ............................................................... 14
How we work in common .................................................................................. 16
Who are your friends? ........................................................................................ 20

**Building a movement** ...................................................................................... 22
DIY – don't wait for permission ........................................................................ 24
Responding to the here and now ..................................................................... 25
Making political theatre .................................................................................... 26
Experimenting with form .................................................................................. 28
Find a common why ........................................................................................... 30
Ripples .................................................................................................................. 31
Press ...................................................................................................................... 33
Chat to people on your street .......................................................................... 33
Pay attention ....................................................................................................... 35
Circular process .................................................................................................. 37
Co-creation – what's that word about? ......................................................... 38
Difficulties – let's be honest ............................................................................. 39

**Sites, ghosts, transformations** ..................................................................... 44
The show starts before you get there ............................................................. 46
Ghosts ................................................................................................................... 47
Touring and being responsive .......................................................................... 50
Layering ................................................................................................................ 52
Building on what's already there | Building with people ........................... 53
Sites-ghosts-transformations ........................................................................... 55

## MAKING

Questions to ask yourself at the start of making ........ 66
How to start a process ........ 67
Stages of a devising process ........ 72
How to lead a warm-up ........ 78
Ways to work with the political body ........ 81
How to make a radical act ........ 84
Transform the space ........ 86
Body mapping ........ 88
Working with modes of address ........ 90
Making up games | Generating images from discussion ........ 91
Simultaneous cards ........ 93
Tasks as prompts for devising ........ 94
Writing prompts ........ 97
Emotional score ........ 99
How to work from a political starting point ........ 101
How to work artistically in a site ........ 104
How to find a site ........ 106
How to interview people ........ 108
How to work from people's experiences ........ 111
How to work in a neighbourhood ........ 112
How to take care ........ 114
How to evaluate ........ 117
Notes on directing ........ 119
Writing political theatre (1) ........ 121
Writing political theatre (2) ........ 125
How to design and build a DIY set ........ 128
How to light people like rock stars ........ 133
Composing and sound design ........ 139
A brief guide to making site-specific theatre ........ 144
How to produce (in a neighbourhood) ........ 150
How to produce (outside of theatre buildings) ........ 154
How to work with young people ........ 159
How to get funding ........ 164
How to tour ........ 172
How to write a press release ........ 175
Ten posh rules ........ 179

# WORKS

Timeline ............................................................................................. 192

## Works – Shows ............................................................................ 198
The Ups and Downs of the Town of Brown (2009) ............................. 200
Our Glass House (2012) ..................................................................... 204
No Guts, No Heart, No Glory (2014) ................................................... 214
The Deal Versus the People (2015) .................................................... 222
We're Still Here (2017) ........................................................................ 228
Radical Acts (2018) ............................................................................. 242
I Have Met the Enemy (and the enemy is us) (2019) ......................... 250
Peaceophobia (2020) .......................................................................... 262
Us Here Now | Reclaim the Space (2022/223) .................................. 272
Off Road (2023) .................................................................................. 282
Fast, Fast, Slow (2023) ....................................................................... 288
Off the Curriculum (2023) .................................................................. 294
We No Longer Talk (2023) .................................................................. 300

## Works – Initiatives ..................................................................... 304
Speakers Corner ................................................................................. 306
The Sounding Board ........................................................................... 312
Youth Theatre Lab .............................................................................. 320
Performance Collective ...................................................................... 326

# AFTERWORD ............................................................................ 334

INDEX ................................................................................................. 336

# CONTRIBUTORS

Casper Ahmed
Shatha Altowai
Camilla Brueton
Simon Casson
Ali Dunican
Alexander Eley
David Evans
Mariyah Kayat
May McQuade
Seherish Mahmood
Ezra Nash
Gary Owen
Jon Pountney
Andy Purves
Catrin Rogers
Wojciech Rusin
Jane Slee
Balvinder Sopal
Mo'min Swaitat
Saoirse Teale
Rachel Trezise
Chantal Williams
Michelle Wren
Aisha Zia

Also, the members of:

Speakers Corner
Common/Wealth Sounding Board
Performance Collective
Youth Theatre Lab

# FOREWORD
Michael Sheen

I write this as the steelworks in my hometown of Port Talbot is going through cataclysmic change. Steelmaking, as we have known it here, has finally come to an end. The iconic blast furnaces have shut down. The last ship has sailed. As a community, we have long feared that this day might come, but the reality of it is still very difficult to process.

A number of times I have found myself thinking back to September of 2017 when I listened to the voices of steelworkers and their families speaking of their fear and anger about the possibility of this very outcome. It was an incredibly powerful experience. Not just because of the power of what they were saying but also because of the context in which they were saying it. This wasn't an edited news report cut down into soundbites, or an amplified speech through a megaphone in the rough chaos of a demonstration.

This was a piece of theatre.

Told in an old, decaying tin works and spoken by the voices of those living through it.

Direct and urgent and unfiltered.

*We're Still Here* was my first experience of the work of Common/Wealth. Commissioned by National Theatre Wales and written by Rachel Trezise in collaboration with the people of Port Talbot, it was inspired by and featured the people behind the 'Save Our Steel' campaign.

Standing among the rest of the audience, some of whom I knew and recognised as fellow members of the local community, some clearly out-of-towners unsure if they had accidentally wandered into some abandoned part of the works by mistake, I had a truly visceral experience. I was moved to tears; I was jolted into anger; I was confronted with a reality that was too easily and too often overlooked or ignored. Too often filtered through the voice of officialdom. Not here – this was from the source, from the heart, from the gut.

It was galvanising.

It demanded a response. People around me made it clear when they agreed or disagreed, added their own takes on what the performers were debating, vocalised their frustrations and their anger. It felt so alive and vital.

It felt like proper theatre.

When you work outside of traditional theatre spaces, a new world of possibilities opens up.

I always remember the words of the great Bill Mitchell, creator of the Cornish site-specific company Wildworks, as we explored potential locations around Port Talbot for our production of *The Passion*. He would make me look around whichever site we were at and say, 'Right! What do we get for free?' He'd make me think about what was already telling a story in that particular environment and how we could use that for our work. How we could work in rhythm with what was around us and release the story already being told.

Everything and everyone is already telling a story.

Only we can speak for us.

The Russian film director Elem Klimov said that you must look for what most needs to be said – which by definition is that which is not being said – and then find a way to say it. This is political theatre stripped to its very core. Its essence.

Part of the power of live performance is that it is a shared experience. A community coming together to share their common values, remember what is of most importance to them, process what is happening to them, where they have come from and explore the possibilities of how to move forward together. And by engaging in that experience, something greater and ultimately mysterious is made possible.

Out of community can come communion.

This does not require anything but the will to make it happen, the audacity to imagine it into being and the courage to see it through.

The book that you hold in your hands is a toolkit.

Find what needs to be said.
Demand a response.
Go to the source.
Move forward together.
Look at what you get for free.

Pick up your tools.
Get to work.

# WHY WE WROTE THIS BOOK

Evie Manning, Rhiannon White
and Jenny Hughes

This book shares the methodology that we have developed over 16 years of work as Common/Wealth, a site-specific, political theatre company based in England and Wales, in the UK. It is for everyone who wants to create performances, art and public events that make a difference to people and places. Whatever your level of experience, we hope this book becomes a practical resource that helps you carry on doing what you're doing.

When we started Common/Wealth we thought theatre could transform the world for the better. We haven't lost hope, and our methodology – the one we share in this book – has become clearer over time. *Do It Yourself: Making Political Theatre* documents the things we've learned from all of our DIY experiments and making do, including practical guidance and exercises we use to develop new work.

We wrote this book because we see the importance of making political theatre now more than ever. Things can feel scary and hopeless, like we're on a runaway train. Right-wing elites controlling our digital worlds in new ways that have an impact on real world events. Occupation, war, conflict, genocide. Floods, fires, extreme weather, fast and furious, out of control. More walls, more borders. Media platforms and politicians acting in ways that are divisive. It's no longer even the political left versus right as much as it is up versus down. Food banks are normalised. Schools, prisons, hospitals, everything swept up by unregulated capitalism. A culture war creating new scapegoats of marginalised people. And we all know this. We watch it play out on our phones. And we don't know what to do about it.

Theatre, for us, is about bringing people together in real life to feel potential, feel change, to challenge the systems around us. We really hope that this book empowers other people to create space for gathering. It doesn't need to be 'theatre' in any recognisable sense. Bring people together, feel your agency and power – this is what we need now. It's necessary and it's not going to be done for us by anyone else. We have to do it ourselves.

## How to use this book

In the book's first section – 'In common' – we write about the principles driving Common/Wealth, with brief illustrations from our work. A section called 'Making' comes next, offering practical exercises, as well as reflections and guidance on making. The final section, 'Works', documents key Common/Wealth shows and initiatives, giving examples of practice and learning from over the course of the company's life.

We wrote this book collectively as a three – Evie, Rhiannon and Jenny. We brainstormed the chapter titles and subtitles, chose them jointly and then set a timer for ourselves to draft each section. Jenny worked to weave these together into something cohesive. We invited other people we work with to contribute their experiences and approaches to making. At first, we were intimidated at the idea of 'writing a book', but our approach was to create it as we would a show – collectively, practically and playfully.

Throughout, we've tried to write in a way that acknowledges our UK context but that will hopefully also be useful to artists and activists across the Global North and South working to create movements for equity and justice.

At the start you'll find the Common/Wealth Manifesto – a statement of how and why we do what we do. You could start there. But we've designed the book to be read however you like. You can read it from beginning to end if you want. Or you could dip in and out of sections – it's up to you. The design has created plenty of space for you to make your own notes, so please go ahead and doodle and scribble wherever you like.

This book is about connecting up and keeping going by sharing the common that is Common/Wealth. Look out for how we did what we did and adapt it – mess about, play, make it fit for your own people and places. Pass it on. Do it your own way.

# Thanks

A massive thank you to everyone who contributed to the making of this book, everyone we've interviewed, everyone we've collaborated with, everyone who has visited us in rehearsals and everyone who has come as audience and stayed to chat after.

And a big thank you to all the people who have supported us as a company along the way, especially Tracy Basu, Hannah Bentley, Sasha Bhat, Devinda Da Silva, Eva Elliot, Patrick Jones, Gary Keogh, Fareeda Khan, Hassan Mahamdallie, Remy Manning, John McGrath, Gerri Moriarty, Michelle Cawardine Palmer, Gavin Porter, Fakhera Rehman, Bobsie Robinson, Saliha Rubani, Ambreen Sadiq, Amer Sarai, Moira Sinclair, Rashmi Sudhir, Alys Taylor, David Taylor, Kae Tempest. Big thanks to our families and partners who have painted walls, moved crap around, stored stuff in attics for decades and had countless conversations about all the personal, professional and political.

Special thanks to our amazing board, past and present, and our brilliant staff teams in Bradford and Cardiff.

Thanks to the people we asked to read the book in draft form, including the anonymous reviewers from Manchester University Press, as well as Ayden Brouwers, Maggie B. Gale, Rabab Ghazoul, Andy Smith, Matt Woodhead. Thanks also to Factory (Manchester) and Canolfan Henblas (Y Bala) for providing venues for our writing retreats, and to Sam Watson for designing the book.

Our work on this book was supported by a UKRI Impact Acceleration Account Award (Jenny Hughes, Common Wealth Theatre & EPSRC UKRI Harmonised IAA 22–26 via University of Manchester – IAA 420).

Biggest thanks to you – the reader – for being interested in our work. We hope that this book is useful to you and that you join the movement for making, seeing and supporting political theatre, and doing it yourself!

# COMMON/WEALTH MANIFESTO

- Fuck capitalism. Fuck theatre. Do it yourself.

- Make shows unlike anything anyone has seen before. Experiment and play with form.

- Don't be afraid of being political. Respond to the here and now. Charge the work with emotion.

- Work with people who have direct experience of the territories you're exploring. They are the creators and editors. Include people new to theatre.

- There is wealth in your experience, your history, your knowledge, where you come from, the stories you get told, stories you pass on.

- Process is as important as form.

- Be an internationalist. Listen and speak beyond borders.

- Get out of theatre buildings. Sites offer so much – they put you in direct conversation with people you wouldn't otherwise meet.

- Work with what you have. Build on what is already there.

- Don't wait for permission. DO IT YOURSELF!

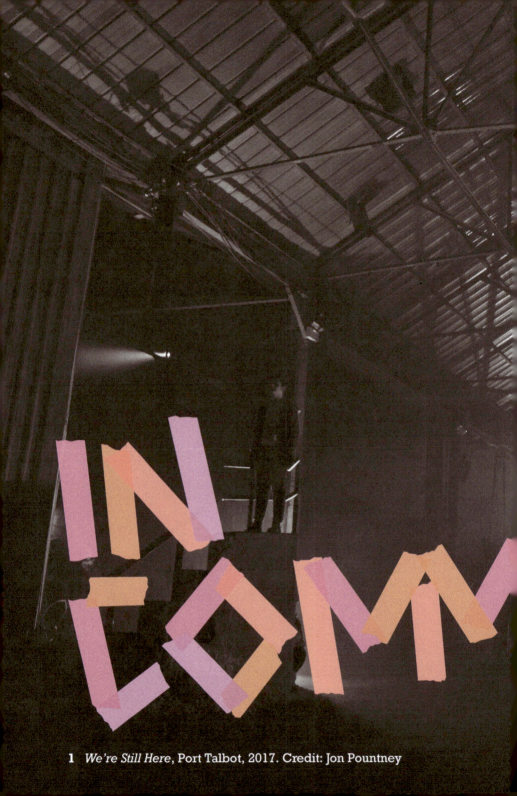

1  *We're Still Here*, Port Talbot, 2017. Credit: Jon Pountney

# WHAT IS COMMON/WEALTH?

***Read on for:*** *what is common?; what is common is wealth; being common; where Common/Wealth comes from; how we work in common; who are your friends?*

We believe in the wealth of being common, of being poor. Working class people are often told they live in 'deprived' areas, but we know first hand how rich these areas are, and how populated they are by people with imagination, opinions and the intention to change things. We always say that our name is TWO words: COMMON, as in – poor, in common, shared; and WEALTH, as in – value, riches. Our work is political and we make art, theatre and performance to build movements for change. It is about reclaiming stories, ideas and space to imagine and create a better world.

We make experimental and political performance that celebrates and reflects the people we know and the places we are from. We have had the best conversations about politics and society with people who are often represented as uninformed, lacking or ill-educated by the mainstream media and theatre. Making experimental performance in working class areas presents all manner of possibilities. From buildings that we can access cheaply to people we can talk to, alongside a 'DIY with whatever you've got' energy, we build friendships with people who have something to say and stories that need to be told.

We started in Bristol in 2008, making work as part of the activist DIY culture scene there at the time, on welfare benefits, working part-time and doing zero-hours contract jobs to get by. We spent time talking about our ideas for theatre, putting the world to rights, writing manifestos. The truth is that we didn't find anything like the art we wanted to see or communities we were part of inside theatre buildings. We adopted a site-specific approach because we were inspired and fascinated by it as a form of theatre, and it brought us closer to people that were familiar and important to us.

Some early performance works attracted attention and we established a reputation for making experimental work in places and with people that do not usually engage with the formal arts scene, touring that work nationally and sometimes internationally. We started to access funding, which meant we could pay ourselves and the people we worked with. And we moved back to the cities we had grown up in – Bradford and Cardiff – slowly but surely getting the company onto a more secure footing, with a board and an administrative and producing team.

Our name, Common/Wealth, is a play on words that says something about how our art gets made. About how we make work from being in common with people, in the places we're from but also, through site-specific touring, connecting to other places. So often in our work, connection comes through sharing a sense of injustice. Whether it be experiences of poverty, discrimination, exploitation, underinvestment, racism, classism, environmental damage, conflict or war – what unites us is an intention to use our knowledge of injustice to connect with others and make the world a better place.

## What is common?

We've worked with steelworkers from Port Talbot, Muslim female boxers from Bradford, teenagers from Chicago, fashion designers from Blackburn and activists from Cardiff. It's all common, baby. And it's all already there, all around you. Sometimes we work with people who have a common interest, skill or job. Sometimes the common is found in shared experiences. Sometimes we find it through working collectively to create a shared intention. The supposedly ordinary and everyday is a territory that we find endlessly interesting. We're big fans of Welsh radical thinker Raymond Williams' assertion that 'culture is ordinary'.[1]

---

[1] Raymond Williams, 'Culture is ordinary', in: Jim McGuigan (ed.), *Raymond Williams on Culture & Society: Essential Writings* (London: Sage, 2013).

The 'creative industries' in the UK, and especially elite sectors like the theatre industry, are dominated by middle class, white, privately educated people. Both in terms of who gets to make art and who comes along to appreciate it. It has become increasingly hard for people from ordinary backgrounds to break through into arts jobs and this has a knock-on effect on storytelling. There are fewer stories about working class communities, and those that exist can often be demeaning and reductive.

Arts and theatre spaces can be alienating and feel weirdly forbidding for us. When we received secure funding from Arts Council England, a high-profile member of the council said, 'Well done, you're middle class now'. Needless to say, we don't see it like that. We know you can be an artist, be educated, be a leader and be working class. The middle classes must be scared. Why else would they want to assimilate everyone into their bullshit?

## What is common is wealth

We start from a place of valuing our experiences and how they have shaped us. We see wealth there and we know that our experiences connect us to each other, through their similarity and their differences. Being common is about being more than one and two, because 'you and me' add up to more than two – there is you, me and this distinct, novel thing that is us – and with every new meeting our common wealth is deepening and expanding. The common is available for all and it's the stuff that connects, the webs and relationships, the threads and fabric that can help us sustain ourselves and each other. It can't be broken up, broken down, itemised, price-tagged, bought and sold. Often, it's about our relationships with things we've forgotten or indeed forgotten to value. Things that anchor, explain, provide purpose, intention, energy.

Valuing the common is not about realising 'assets' in our 'deficit' communities. We resist thinking of ourselves as worthy of 'investment' that will 'pay dividends', 'appreciate' or 'pay off' over time. The structural inequities in our communities won't be salved or solved by art projects. Things can only change by building coalitions and movements that challenge injustice in a fundamental way. People who live in the places we come from and work in are used to being told they're not good enough, not worth enough. Our places struggle with the impact of long-term underinvestment, and no amount of theatre shows are going to change that.

Think about who you are and what's around you now, but also think back. Think small and think big. Think about the miniature things that are rich in meaning, but also think about the epic and awesome. Your common wealth is not just about us as in you and me, our parents, this house, on this estate. It's also about longer and older stories. It's about why things are the way they are, and what was lost along the way, as well as the things that seem to have disappeared but still exist, if we look for them. Why are you so determined? How did your cousin come to love drawing and be so good at it? Why are the streets in your area named after trees, artists, other places? How did your neighbour set up that dance club for kids from her kitchen with no money? What about those people who run the social centre down the road – what's their story? What's the story behind the way there is a border between your place and the places next door? Your town and the town next door? This country and the country next door? There's so much that has gone into who you are, and your possibility, and it is all there, available, ready to be told and retold, discovered and shaped anew.

There's an exercise we love to do at the start of a creative process which is about sharing what we're good at. We create a collective playlist of all the songs we love to dance to and play a game where we dance until the music stops. Then we tell the person next to us what we're really good at.

We invite you to put on some music, have a dance, sit with a piece of paper and write down what your wealth is.

## Being common

Here are our personal stories of being common, shared here in case it helps those of you who – like us – have found yourselves the only one a bit like you in an art space:

**Evie:** 'Wherever we go, people always ask us, who we are and where do we come from, and then we always tell them, we come from Bradford, shitty, shitty Bradford' – school bus chant.

There's something about being a kid and the whole world being the five streets around you. We were out all day and night and every bit of space had a story. As kids, we had this collective history, the witch's house, the brothel, the drug dealer's car, the garden you're allowed to play in, the houses you break into, the roses you always nick. And then as a teenager the city gets bigger and places take on a different kind of symbolism. The road where your friend was found dead, the flat where you skived school, the place you were when the riots happened, the nightclubs that let you in, where you got in that fight, the times you walked home from town because you couldn't afford the taxi fare. It's all those places and stories that form who you are. I left for eight years and coming back home, you realise that all those layers, all those ghosts are still there. It's a reminder of why you do creative work. You know it's important to set up opportunities for young people who are growing up in a city with all these stories, and not all of them good.

My high school deputy head called me and my friends 'cheap, common tarts from Bradford town who would never go anywhere in life'. 'I expect to see you pushing a pram around town within a year', she said. We were 15 years old and laughed it off but that word 'common' stuck with me. I went to study theatre at Goldsmiths, University of London, because my friend applied for me and I knew I needed to get away from Bradford. I'd had too much heartache and been started on too many times. Goldsmiths turned me down at the interview stage (I'd been up all night the night before because my boyfriend told me he was going to prison for assault – I spent the coach journey crying, trying to sleep). In the end I got straight A grades and got in through clearing. It always pissed me off that my grades were good enough but I wasn't - my make up, my clothes, my gobbinness, and when I started I felt my class for one of the first times.

At university I was very 'Bradford' among girls my age from the Home Counties, really middle class, sheltered, with Backstreet Boys posters on their walls - or upper class and privately educated. There were 60 kids on the degree and I was one of the few who had a regional accent. In my first week, when I first put my hand up to speak, a lecturer said, in front of the whole year, 'I'm sorry dear, but I didn't understand a word you just said'. And the whole lecture hall laughed.

I felt different and simultaneously like I should be there, to disrupt it all. I felt like I'd lived a life. I'd been going out clubbing since I was 14, known a lot of people who had died between the ages of 14 and 18, and felt older than my years. The riots in Bradford happened when I was 17 and I saw friends get harsh sentences, police violence and injustice coming into sharp focus. Going to university and seeing all these posh kids who seemed so privileged and distant from what I'd grown up with made me angry and aware of what class really meant. I resisted the course for a while but, in the end, it offered me creative freedom and a chance to be myself in a way that Bradford couldn't. But that anger at the massive gap between classes, rich and poor, stayed with me.

I stayed in London for a few years after graduating – it was so different to Bradford and I wasn't ready to go back. I squatted buildings as a way to afford to live in the city and self-organised parties and performances. It was mainly pretty scrappy but always very political. We had a wall in the first pub we squatted where people had to write their manifesto when they came in.

Squatting is a philosophy, anti-capitalist, transformative – always do it yourself.

I was 26 years old when I got pregnant with my son, Remy, and knew I would be a single parent. My mum had been a single parent to three kids and still maintained her art practice as a printmaker, so I knew it could be done. At seven months pregnant I moved back into my old room at my mum's house in Bradford, searching for purpose. I had a meeting with the studio theatre at the university and asked if I could have a space to set up a youth theatre. The artistic director there told me to forget about it, that I probably wouldn't want to do anything for five years until my child was bigger. That kind of undermining fuelled me, and when Remy was six months old I moved to Bristol to make one of our first shows, *Our Glass House*.

I was lucky because Remy was such a good sleeper. He'd sleep for three hours during the day and I'd work on Common/Wealth, registering us as a company, building the website, writing funding bids. We took Remy everywhere, to meetings, workshops. My friend would take him on walks during rehearsal and bring him back to be breastfed. He was one year old while we cleaned and decorated for *Our Glass House*, sitting in his pram in the garden while we scrubbed the house. I was on benefits until he was eight, when we became an Arts Council England–funded National Portfolio organisation. I was so determined to make it all work. Almost to prove I could.

I always encourage people to access all the benefits they can get to support them to be an artist and not feel any shame about that. Benefits are designed to support people. You're part of a long line of artists who've used benefits to survive and make art. And bringing children along with you is part of your survival as an artist and a person. Remy has been along for the ride all the way – he's been part of political workshops at Speakers Corner since he was five, performed in shows, been on tour with us. It's enriched his life and mine and Common/Wealth's having him there.

**Rhiannon:** I come from St Mellons, a council estate on the edge of Cardiff, a place that carries a historic narrative of poverty and crime. My mum was one of the first to get a council house there and was so chuffed. It was something to be proud of – your house with a garden and three bedrooms. St Mellons was a 1970s housing development built on former farmland, and bad planning left the area with very little. It became famous for vilified single mums, shopping in Tesco in their pyjamas, high-profile murders and the incredible grassroots dance collective The Underdogs, which Chantal, who now works for Common/Wealth, ran with her mum, Roberta.

It's rare to find anyone working in theatre who comes from a place like mine. The industry is overrun with people who can afford to leap into the uncertain world of trying to make a living from art. The quietly confident, financially stable, cushioned individuals who can afford to live in the big cities, who speak the language, have the networks and the education.

Our street was a series of tightly packed houses, a semi-circle interconnected with gullies and underpasses. Every inch of our street was used for something – we claimed every nook and cranny, kids playing games passed down through generations: hide and seek, ratatat ginger, bulldogs. Mums and dads sat on the council-installed bollards and front steps, nattering, drinking tea, sharing food. People beavering away in their gardens, doing up battered old cars. Windows were held open, with sound systems blasting out reggae, bass turned up. Sounds clashed as the music from the speakers of opposite houses met from either side of the street, a standoff between who had the loudest. All against the backdrop of council signs drilled into the sides of houses, 'no ball games allowed'.

Our street lost many people to drug overdoses. There were weekly fights – men with machetes were not an unusual sight. So many people had experienced domestic violence. Among it all, I grew up knowing that people had my back. Neighbours, friends – we knew what it felt like to be treated like shit. I grew up in a violent household, and that experience – where you're the one responsible for picking up the pieces and making sense of it all – instilled in me a fight against injustice. From a young age, I had to speak up and speak out.

I had an amazing teacher, Mr Walsh, who took us on trips, including to gigs, and I got to see lots of alternative culture. Aged 15, looking for a new job, I trawled the telephone directory, phoning cafes. I got to C and phoned Chapter Arts Centre. I had never been there before. Come in for an interview, they said, we're looking for someone. I got two buses to the centre. They gave me a job and, all of a sudden, I was in another world, still an outsider but immersed in experimental performance and film, rubbing shoulders with some of the best contemporary artists in Wales.

When I was 16, I saw Patrick Jones' play, *Everything must go*, and that really spoke to my life. It was about being Welsh. There was unemployment, drugs, self-harm, depression – sadly those things felt very familiar. But it was also laced with this Welsh history that I didn't know. Aneurin Bevan, socialism – teaching me about ordinary people being able to do things, not just in the theatre, but also politically. I'd felt ashamed of being Welsh, being from a council estate and going to a shit school, but this play made me feel different. Like I could do it, like so many who had come before. In Wales we're literally standing on the shoulders of giants.

I studied theatre at Dartington because my college teacher, Meryl, recommended it. She had studied there. She said, 'The things you like – that's what is taught at Dartington'. I didn't have anyone to give me a lift, so Clive, the security guard from Chapter, dropped me off. Everyone thought he was my dad.

At Dartington, it was predominantly wealthy kids with a theatre hobby. All the kids who came from backgrounds like mine became a little gang. We spent a lot of time not knowing what to do in studio sessions where we were left alone to 'make work' – but in a way that was the making of us, helping us be free, learning how to make it up and do it ourselves. There were so many distractions when I was at Dartington, with my mum still in an abusive relationship. Baggage came with me and stayed through that time. It was quite hard to switch between those two worlds. It still is.

In my twenties, I joined Circus 2 Palestine, a group of self-organised, DIY clowns taking circus to the Middle East. For around four years I travelled to and from the West Bank and eventually Gaza. We took our shows to rooftops, schools, houses, community centres. We had a grassroots network of friends, women's groups, NGOs and children's groups, often seven of us sleeping in someone's front room, making it up as we went along, trying to reach as many children as possible. We forged letters in Arabic to cross the border into Gaza, impromptu performances for Egyptian and Palestinian border guards at Rafah Crossing helping us to cross a military no-go zone.

In Palestine, I learned how the arts play a role in cultural resistance and how they can be transformative for people and a lifeline in times of war. I made lifelong friends with people fighting to keep culture alive while keeping themselves and their families intact. I took all that learning home with me. I remember this life-changing moment, two days after getting home from Gaza. I was at a rave in the Welsh mountains on army training land. I sat on the floor with my boyfriend at the time, sobbing, telling him about how in Gaza people were dying to live and here in the UK people were living to die. Surrounded by spent bullets and cartridges, with the army running laps around us. It was surreal. That was when I gave up getting fucked up and got seriously focused on making theatre.

## Where Common/Wealth comes from

Common/Wealth was formed in Bristol in 2008. The city's DIY culture provided the nursery ground for our early pieces and a gang of people to work with. Bristol felt like a land of opportunity, with massive empty buildings, a powerful squatting movement, lively club and festival circuit, and artists and activists doing it themselves en masse. Semi-derelict buildings provided perfect venues for us to meet, talk, play, party, connect with others – most not part of the theatre scene at all – and make our first shows.

With the gentrification of Bristol city centre and surrounding neighbourhoods, much of this has gone. Our former base is now a boutique hotel.

As time moved on, we also saw how the two sides of the city we connected with didn't really see each other. White middle class activists and multiracial working class communities struggling with the impact of austerity. We might have established Common/Wealth in Bristol, but we chose to leave, creating bases in our hometowns of Bradford and Cardiff.

Bradford is the sixth biggest city in the UK and 29% of the population are under 20 years old. Following the success of *Our Glass House* (see 'Works'), Evie wanted to return home and to represent the city differently to how it was perceived. There was a sense of Common/Wealth finding a purpose and making a difference to a place that had nurtured you and the people you knew. Being in Bradford, Common/Wealth received a small, regular pot of funding from the local authority, and the many empty buildings in the city centre meant that it was cheap to bring a company together.

Common/Wealth has had a physical base in Bradford since 2014. At the time of writing, our current home, Common Space, is in a former youth opportunity centre in the corner of the old indoor market with an incredibly leaky roof. Our rent is cheap but we can be evicted at a week's notice. Despite its difficulties, Common Space offers the kind of creative space that artists working in cities with higher real estate values can only dream of.

The drawback of Bradford is its distance – not so much in kilometres, but in imagination – from metropolitan centres like London and Manchester. It's difficult to get press to review our non-touring shows and difficult for us to connect with others doing experimental and political work. Artists tend not to come to Bradford and lack of investment means that there is only a small artist scene. As is typical for places experiencing long-term underinvestment, the arts scene in the city is kept in a perpetual state of 'emergence'.

Inspired by what was happening in Bradford, Rhiannon returned home to Cardiff, working initially in partnership with visiting artists and companies. In 2024, as we were writing this book, the company secured portfolio funding from the Arts Council of Wales. The other draw of Cardiff was the first few years of National Theatre Wales (established in 2007), which saw the lineage of experimental work that Rhiannon had been part of as a teenager developed in what felt like an ambitious and meaningful way. With the establishment of National Theatre Wales and the ambition of its first artistic director, John McGrath, it felt like things were possible in Wales. There were more jobs in the arts and Welsh theatre was back on the map.

The draw of home had always been strong, through many years of moving from show to show in neighbourhoods like her own but not her own. Rhiannon was curious about what would happen if she took all that learning and confidence and applied it to a context she knew well. As luck would have it, an old pub on the same road as her mum's first council house was in the process of being renovated as a community asset, and it had office space for rent. It provided the perfect home, situated right in the heart of an estate that she knew so well.

## How we work in common

Common/Wealth operates across two different sites, in two different cities, in two different countries. We work from the same mission, vision and values, and we share internal operations – things like finance, policies and governance. Evie heads up Bradford and Rhiannon heads up Cardiff. You could say we're a devolved theatre company, with a central constitution and creative activity across the two sites. Our company make-up means that we work with two different arts councils – Arts Council England and the Arts Council of Wales. The arts councils are our key funder in each site, and each has distinct priorities and processes.

This throws up challenges. How do we make sure our board understands both places? How do we tell the story of both places on social media? How do we sort out our finances? We're fuelled by the two places we work in, and the connections that are forged within and between each place feel exciting. Working class communities so often face the same struggles. Our places are unique but have a lot in common, both with each other and with places facing injustice elsewhere in the world. Working across two places keeps us rooted in that.

Everything about running the company has a politics and we've shaped that together, so our values and approach in each location are the same. We have a shared 'why' for all elements of the company. We exist as a political theatre company and our politics shape what we do and say and put out into the world, how we are funded, how we pay our staff, performers and young people. We employ people who get the politics, who are compassionate, who are up for having political conversations about everything from the genocide in Palestine to the rise of the far right. Our solid purpose grounds us and is a guiding light when we have to make difficult decisions or sort out disputes.

We're often asked how co-artistic leadership of the company works. When we met in Bristol, we connected with each other over our class anger, our love for experimental performance and our politics. We respected and trusted each other – we had grown up in similar circumstances and there was a shorthand between us. It was like finding a kindred spirit and we knew to invest in that. From that foundation, we were able to be brave in our decisions and we helped each other to be even braver. We spent those early days plotting, devising, vibing off each other, and our passion, ambition and values all clicked.

Our relationship over the years has been one of bouncing ideas around and never being scared to say the obvious or the obscure thing. We spend hours hashing out ideas before they make it to the rehearsal room. In rehearsals Evie can be more impulsive, trying things out on the spot; Rhiannon observant, seeing what lands. As a creative relationship it really works. Rhiannon's a thinker and planner and processor; Evie's a doer, fast-moving, finding her feet in the moment. Rhiannon is good at digging into the story. Evie is good at making decisions, getting to the heart of it. We both have a talent for building relationships and we love the process of discovering a show.

Over time, we each wanted to follow this desire to make things happen in the places we come from. With the geographical distance, we haven't made a piece of work together for some time and we miss each other a lot in a physical way. We still brainstorm ideas and challenge and bounce things around with each other – and when the time is right, we'll make a piece of work as a whole company. Our love for the work and for each other has helped us navigate our differences. We don't always get it right. What has worked for us is being brave enough to face the hard bits head-on. Being able to question, challenge and hold each other to account, keep our egos in check and become a united force when needed.

Most recently, we've had challenging discussions about our name – Common/Wealth – what it means, how it resonates, whether we need to change it. Especially given the global movement against systemic racism and racist violence and the need to engage with legacies of British colonialism. We chose the name Common/Wealth because we identified with anti-austerity, social justice campaigns that actively resist the demonisation and stigmatisation of the 'poor'. But we know that the name does not always translate well internationally. Artists and activists from postcolonial and Commonwealth countries have asked questions about it. For some, the word 'Commonwealth' featured on the cover of their schoolbooks alongside an image of the British crown. The 'Commonwealth' is part of a long history of uninvited British intervention across the world, a history that has led to powerful calls for reparations that continue to be ignored (at best) and fiercely resisted (at worst) here in Britain. We back calls for reparation and we want our work to actively support ongoing anticolonial global justice movements.

We also chose Common/Wealth because we were inspired by the idea of the 'commons' – an idea rooted in a commitment to share resources fairly and a recognition that resources for living well belong to everyone. By 'resources', commons thinkers mean material things like land, food and the natural environment, homes and institutions, neighbourhoods and streets, as well as more abstract things like ideas, art, language, relationships, memories, identities and feelings. Commons thinking is present in many different localities across the world and has inspired generations of activists.[2] We're also inspired by these ideas, and the ingenious, inventive, generous people and places they connect to, all creating space and time for dreaming, playing, talking and listening, sharing, celebrating and interrogating alternatives to rampant unregulated capitalism.

Common/Wealth is a white-led company and we work consciously to reach beyond the limitations this creates. As part of this, we are continuously thinking about solidarity building against capitalism and all forms of oppression. We know how necessary it is for working class people to join together.

---

[2] If you're interested in knowing more, we recommend Guy Standing's *Plunder of the Commons: A Manifesto for Sharing Public Wealth* (London: Pelican, 2019). For a more practical book, try J. K. Gibson-Graham, Jenny Cameron, Stephen Healy, *Take Back the Economy: An Ethical Guide for Transforming our Communities* (Minneapolis, MN: University of Minnesota Press, 2013).

## Who are your friends?

Everyone knows the old boys' club, but we made the new girls' club. Every time you make a play, you form a gang. Alice Nutter, writer and former member of the band Chumbawamba, shared that idea with us. You form a gang and you have to back your gang and not be afraid to challenge your gang. The gang feeling is powerful, walking down the street knowing you've got a shared purpose. Your gang have their contacts, so make your gang porous and able to grow. That way you can form networks of people who support what you're doing and will back you and champion you and introduce you to their mates who will bring their own gang down to the show.

Your process, the people you know and the experiences you've had, your stories, your language and your style, are your wealth. People will trust you and want to help you because of who you are and how you communicate. If you're upper class, you might know someone who knows the director general of the BBC or you go to dinner parties with lawyers and doctors. Our gangs and our networks are different but no less important. Someone on your street owns three quad bikes you can use in a show, or you have a friend who can spread the word across a whole estate. We always sell out in our home cities of Bradford and Cardiff and our audiences are predominantly working class. Many have never been to theatre in their lives, beyond our plays. That's because of our networks.

Invite people into the making process, people who are curious about what's going on, have something to say, know something useful or have a stake in the storytelling. People who can bring different perspectives. We work to a principle of, if you're in the room, you're part of the process. From the person dropping off the boxes to the friend who's wandered in because they saw someone they know. Maybe they can teach you a song or know where you can find some shopping trolleys.

The work – the shows, our approach – has travelled to national and international cities as well as across colleges, universities, campaigns, movements, social organisations, charities and businesses. We make new friends wherever we go. We work with anyone who recognises that things are not working for everyone, that it is possible to make them better, and sees a place for theatre-making in the changes that need to happen. The borders of our work are open. If you've heard of us, and you're on board with the idea of theatre and change, you are part of the wealth of the common. You're part of a network that includes

the boxing coaches,
the landladies,
the loudmouths who know the whole place,
the pub singers,
the union reps,
the teenage girls,
the school teachers,
the right-on council leaders,
the community centres,
the librarians,
the school governors,
the university lecturers,
the anarchists,
the lunch clubs,
the old people's homes,
the domestic violence charities,
the gangsters,
the dealers,
the recovering drug addicts,
the former soldiers turned Buddhist,
the hungry-for-change single mums,
the worried parents,
the youth workers,
the boys on quad bikes,
the teacher who gave up her job to set up a drama club on the
    estate …

# BUILDING A MOVEMENT

***Read on for:*** *DIY – don't wait for permission; responding to the here and now; making political theatre; experimenting with form; find a common why; ripples; press; chat to people on your street; pay attention; circular process; co-creation – what's that word about?; difficulties – let's be honest*

Theatre can build movements and create a sense that change is possible. It can reset the dial on popular opinion. In the political mainstream, there is widespread acceptance of capitalism and the inequalities it produces, and a refusal to reckon with the legacies of colonial violence that are so embedded in the DNA of many countries. We see making and watching performance as something that can tap into our dreams and imagination and show us that another world is possible, and it always was. We see theatre-making as creating a space to:

- Imagine the world differently
- Connect with people
- Build solidarity
- Offer hope

We connect with existing campaigns at every stage of making, engaging with activists to ensure the process is rooted in the knowledge and experience of those already doing transformative work. Our shows often support specific campaigns. We research who is out there making change in the territory we're working in. They'll have been doing this work long before we've made a show and will carry on long after. We've worked with Campaign Against the Arms Trade, Trade Justice Movement, JENGbA (Joint Enterprise Not Guilty by Association), Save Our Steel, The Revival (Ghana), Women's Aid and many local domestic abuse organisations. We're one part of a bigger movement, playing a role through the theatre we make. We can't do this work in isolation.

We believe in being activated by and activating our audiences, building a movement through our cast, audiences, our own company and its networks and people that know our work.

Our communities have experienced multiple injustices that intersect with one another. They are at the sharp end of it all. We bring people together in spaces where they meet, talk, see each other, create and work out what they want to say. We use theatre to platform topics that don't normally get represented in politics or the media, and people who aren't normally heard. We know we need a movement to amplify the presence of working class people and create solidarity across communities and across distances. To get people feeling not so alone.

Building a movement happens with the crew you bring together, the audience who come, the ripples from the show, the press it generates, the campaigns that link up, the stories that get told, the people who reach out afterwards. The work naturally builds movement. We bring people together, unlikely relationships are born and a sense of momentum is palpable.

It builds the common that is wealth. That's what theatre can do. It's why we wanted to write this book. If you're reading this, you're part of a movement which says yes, steal these exercises, borrow this and that, occupy your space and do it your own way. This doesn't belong to us – none of it does. And we want more people making political theatre that challenges entrenched ideas of how the world should be.

## DIY – don't wait for permission

Go ahead. Do it anyway. Common/Wealth arose from our sense that the work couldn't wait. What that meant is that we didn't care about the theatre industry, how to enter it or how to become recognised.

We don't wait for permission. We find networks of people who want to make, create, act and live differently. When we started the company, the people we found and the people who found us had learned how to clean up empty, derelict sites and transform them into performance spaces. We knew people who could build electricity rigs from lamp posts, who could rewire, who could create beautiful, intricate sets out of cardboard, who knew how to make places safe, and had time to imagine and build things from nothing.

We made theatre in the spaces we found and with whatever we had to hand. We still carry that ethos. It's not about money or buildings. It's about the way we are with people and spaces.

Don't wait for permission. You don't need a studio or a theatre to make work. Use your living room, the church hall, the community centre, the street, the park. Get a group of mates together and know that you are the most important resource. One of you will know how to hook up a projector, another how to get the sound system working. One of you will be stronger with music choices, another with text, another with visuals. Get talking, have the idea, build it together.

The theatre industry in the UK at the time of writing is in a steep decline. Theatre buildings and programmers are risk averse, recycling the classics to put bums on seats, and new work isn't getting championed. It feels even more important to make work on the edges, to do it differently. Use your tools and anything and everything you have to hand to get the work out there. The idea is the most important thing and we need new ideas more than ever.

Build it and they will come. Once you've got the show together, flyer the neighbours, your friends, the shops. Don't have money for a sound system or to print flyers? Beg, steal, borrow. Put a call out, use your networks, do it through socials. Don't be afraid for things to look hand-drawn or hand-made. That's your aesthetic right now and it's beautiful. Also, don't lose it, even when you get money or funding. Continue being resourceful – keep thinking of what you can borrow, steal and recycle.

## Responding to the here and now

Making theatre is our way of responding to the world in the here and now. It's our way of helping ourselves and other people feel equipped to face the challenges of living in an increasingly unstable world. Decisions are made at levels that are unreachable. Algorithms create unrest and division. The elites are scared of us, in our multitudes, in our commonality and differences, and dedicate effort to making sure we are fighting among ourselves. It's easy to feel apathy and despair. We love people, we believe in people, and see our power and potential every day. We also see and experience how complicated and knotty people are. As are the challenges we face.

Idealism and anger in equal measure fuel us a lot of the time. But we don't sit still. We always want to respond, react, and we try to do so quickly, with the shifting political ground – whether that's staging a reading of the Gaza Monologues,[3] mobilising our networks in the face of unimaginable genocide in Palestine, creating a car-meet in response to 'Punish a Muslim Day' (*Radical Acts*), putting on self-defence classes when there is fear of far-right extremism (*Speakers Corner*), or making a show about the British arms trade (*I Have Met the Enemy*). We don't go quietly into the night (see 'Works' for more on these shows and initiatives).

We think of art and culture as a necessity and as a right. Our work is honest and real, emotional and personal. It brings the here and now into reach. It makes change feel possible.

## Making political theatre

'Political', in its simplest form, means power – and there's power in voice, in being heard, in telling your own story, taking focus and paying attention to people and places that are ignored. We get

---

[3] Gaza Monologues is a project initiated by Ashtar Theatre in Palestine. Monologues originally written by young people in Gaza after Israel's military incursion in 2010 have been performed in more than 80 cities and 40 countries in solidarity with people in Palestine. To find out how to stage your own, visit gazamonologues.com (accessed 10 January 2025).

people who have not had access to political platforms or decision-making forums into positions of power in our performances. But we hate it when people talk about 'the voiceless'. Everyone has a voice – they just need to be listened to. Making political theatre is an open-ended process. You pay attention, respond, create something, send it out, create ripples; people respond, the ripples keep growing and narratives keep changing, and bit by bit we're part of a collective process of change.

Theatre can provide a platform for what's not getting spoken about and feels dangerous to say in public spaces. You can get away with saying a lot in theatre, and it can be a rallying space. We're living in times characterised by ignoring and forgetting, and we believe that theatre has a role in paying attention to the world we live in now. It's as simple as that. We believe all theatre is political. Every choice in theatre is a choice between paying attention or perpetuating our traditions of ignoring, forgetting and looking away.

Because our work is political, people's experiences are at the centre. As we've said, we started the company partly as a reaction against a middle class art world that didn't reflect the people we know. But we're never trying to show the broken bits of people and places because it's more dramatic that way. We work with people's actual experiences, their complexities, and bring them into a creative process where they imagine, experiment, make it up, try things out. Ending up with something that celebrates and enhances the wealth of the common, and that also allows people to share safely, have new experiences, enjoy themselves and connect across differences.

Our sources of inspiration are experimental performance, live art practice, theatres of the political left, and the activist culture of the global justice movement. We borrow from and play with approaches connected to all of these sources. But we're not on board with the intellectualising that can dominate contemporary theatre practice. We're not interested in the separation of theatre into categories – 'experimental', 'socially engaged', 'community, 'political' – and we're uncomfortable with experimental art that sits inside bland corporate spaces, far from the places we're from.

## Experimenting with form

Every time we make a show, we try to make something we've never seen before and that we think an audience hasn't seen before. That's a big ask, and maybe impossible, but it's a nice motivator. We've never been into traditional staging or 'acting' or 'beginning, middle, end', so that frees us up straight away. We create atmospheres, environments and worlds, using sound, visuals and awareness of the audience's journey. We like to have a clear vision that we can work with, and during the process we play endlessly with stuff – objects, ideas, stories – whatever is in the world around us. Bringing things into the room as we discover them, responding to the people and place throughout.

We challenge assumptions relating to what working class people might want from theatre. We introduce people to experimental form and love seeing how the work connects deeply, through its creation of atmosphere, politics and feeling.

The experimentation is different with each show. Sometimes the site leads. How can we play a derelict tin factory like a musical instrument (*We're Still Here*)? What does occupying city hall look like (*The Deal Versus the People*)? Sometimes the content drives it; sometimes it's a new design element. With *Off the Curriculum*, experimentation was at the heart of a process which followed young people as they were provided with space, time and resources to design their own learning experience (see 'Works' for more on these shows).

The drive to experiment informs who we bring on board. We tend to prefer working with artists and musicians rather than set and sound designers from mainstream theatres. That way, you're in a territory where you're finding the visual and sonic world and not necessarily the 'story'. It allows for the world you're making to be the thing.

We're drawn to experimental form because the show does not have to make 'sense' in a way that can patronise an audience. People have their own minds and they don't need us telling them what to think. We leave lots of space around the images, gestures, atmospheres and phrases we're playing with in a scene and in the overall structure of a show – pauses for people to land, breath, feel, make their own connections. Working with collage-like structures that don't tie it all up neatly means that people have an experience, follow their own associations, make their own meanings. Getting a boxer to run up and down the gym for ages before making a big speech creates so much feeling because you're with her physically (*No Guts, No Heart, No Glory*). She's tired, sweating and out of breath. You share a real moment with her.

As might be obvious by this point in the book, our primary sources of inspiration are the people around us and the places we come from. But we're also influenced and inspired by the work of other artists, especially artists that work with concepts rather than narrative or conventional dramatic form, and that also work to transform community and build solidarity and interrogation. These artists include Tania El Khoury, Theaster Gates, Forensic Architecture, Brith Gof, Bertolt Brecht, Welfare State International, the Freedom Theatre, fix+foxy, Lung Theatre, Touretteshero. As a company, we've worked closely with the Berlin-based collective Gob Squad, sharing our practices with each other, and we're especially inspired by their use of the 'four Rs' – reality, rhythm, rules, risk (check out their book, *Gob Squad and the Impossible Attempt to Make Sense of It All*[4]).

---

[4] *Gob Squad and the Impossible Attempt to Make Sense of It All* (Berlin: Gob Squad, 2015). Available from: https://www.gobsquad.com/product/gob-squad-and-the-impossible-attempt-to-make-sense-of-it-all/ (accessed 10 January 2025).

When making a show, we think a lot about the audience's journey. We want the experience to be immersive and emotional and not too intellectual, because we think that's the best way to bring the political into reach. We are not interested in telling people what to think and feel, but we do want to create experiences that generate opportunities for people to think and feel, forge new associations, and where they can share their responses. If you land the audience in feeling, it relays the political in human scale. It triggers a feeling and connection rather than demanding a judgement from you or making a judgement about you.

## Find a common why

Taking on a political subject can feel daunting – how do you make it relate to people's experience? With much of our work we start with a political theme: the arms trade, trade justice, the destruction of industry, fast fashion, police injustice. We go deep with our research, absorbing everything we can, and all this feeds the why of the show.

Think deep and wide. What's the point of telling this story right now, and in this way? It needs to matter in ways that extend outwards. The key thing about making political theatre is that it's got to be more than just for you. So ask yourself, who is it for? Why does it matter? Why would the audience get on board?

You need to get your collective on board with the why. Ask the questions: why are you making it? What are you trying to achieve, to explore? What do you want the audience to feel? Everyone needs to understand the answers to those questions, so that you're all working towards a common why.

Sometimes when we're working with people who are performing from their own experience, and who have never performed before, the show becomes their big moment. Which it can be, of course, but that can make them vulnerable and exposed or even full of ego, and their experience can start to overshadow other people's. Establishing a common why can help with this. Return to questions like: why are we making this piece? Why are we telling this story? What's the bigger picture? What are we trying to achieve? Understanding the why helps everyone become better curators and editors. You can keep coming back to it when you're struggling to make a decision or find a way through.

The common why is a holding space for intentions, images, conversations, relationships and moments. It helps everyone to distil and filter, to access the kernel of a show. It shines a guiding light through the process.

## Ripples

When we make a political performance, we want its impact to be so much bigger than the show itself. The ripple effect created by a show isn't something that simply comes afterwards. It's a constant, evolving motion that is there from the start. When we start each show, we catch hold of something that seems interesting or important, and the ripples circle back, creating channels, flows and cross-currents that build in ways that are impossible to predict.

The fact that the show exists can create ripples on its own. People hear about it and take notice and think, great, someone made a show about that. Someone could be reading about the show 200 kilometres away and still connect to it. Sometimes because of its audacity. It can start conversations and give people the sense that they're not the only one feeling that way. There are local, national and international ripples and there are also more intimate connections. Quiet conversations about a scene, a feeling that lands and stays for a while, a phrase or a gesture that becomes part of your personal armoury.

Because we think about our plays as campaigns, we work with agencies and across networks. It's how we get the message out. Getting a feature in a housing association newsletter, union newspaper, or on local radio can be massively important, as it means the messages from the play are being thought and spoken about beyond the show.

We aim for every show to be an hour long. If you can't say it in an hour, what are you doing? Shorter shows leave more space for the important things that happen afterwards. Our shows can stir up a lot in an audience and often they want to stay to chat. After each show we create opportunities so the audience doesn't experience a hard end to the experience; they can linger in the world of the show, returning to their everyday life gradually. Sometimes audiences need to be together for a minute to catch their breath. Or to ask questions about what to do next. To take space and time to decompress and digest.

We document what we do and, by documenting, try to spread the ripples further. This might take the form of a report or a film. Documentation creates space for new connections to rise to the surface. A campaign group sees the film and asks if they can use it in their training; a report informs local strategic work.

We don't know what impact the work has. Social scientists have come up with so many ways to measure impact, but there's a great deal of disagreement about how to do it. Research methods can't capture the complex processes of creative and collaborative making in sites that don't stand still long enough for you to get your (qualitative or quantitative) tape measure out. The pressure to evaluate is there, but the way change happens comes down to individual and collective agency in conditions not of our choosing. We try not to narrow down what 'positive' change looks like in our evaluations, and instead ask questions with the people who have been part of the movement. Figuring out what worked and the learning to take forward. We are open to changes that look small, and the significance of ripples that pass by without anyone noticing at first.

## Press

Find a good press officer. It's one of the best pieces of advice we ever got. You're going to have to pay them. Get to know them and help them get to know the show and why you're making it. Talk about the bigger picture, the social and political messages the show connects with. Pay attention to what is happening in the news right now. Be savvy. Use your contacts – your friend with the online blog, that friend of a friend who knows a journalist, and ask them to pitch for you. You need people who will help your story, your message, your intention to travel to the armchair of the dad in front of the telly. Or the phone of the young girl in her bedroom. Working with a good press officer can get theatre people interested and bring audiences. Most importantly, good press creates airtime for the subject matter of your show.

Attracting press is hard, especially if you live outside of major cities. Although there are brilliant theatre critics out there, many in the UK press tend to see through the lens of London theatre. This means that when you're making work beyond a critic's everyday experience, they sometimes don't get it or believe in it or even see what you see. So, when you get press, read it with a critical eye, and don't necessarily believe the good or the bad. Think – what are the bits that connect with what you're trying to achieve? Sing about them. The bits where they didn't get you? Dig into that and sit with it. Is that what it looks like from the outside? Reviews can be painful but they open your show up for discussion. You can read them or not read them, agree or disagree with them. But know that even if your work ends up in a right-wing rag, at least it got someone talking, or affronted, and that's great.

## Chat to people on your street

Here's what our Community Producer, Chantal Williams, wrote about building an audience for a show:

East Cardiff. A concrete jungle of terraced houses in juxtaposition to nature. A place where drug dealing is an entrepreneurial skill misdirected and volunteers litter pick. It's a community of passion, little opportunity, shit education and crime. It is also home, filled with character, stories, histories and battles. When I'm in theatre industry rooms where people are throwing out about diversifying their audience and targeting the demographic of those who don't engage with the arts, I think about Mary who bakes cakes on a Sunday and shouts at me for parking in the wrong spot. Mary doesn't give a shit about your show. The question should be what do they want to see, rather than how can we get people to come to what we have decided they would like to see. If you're not asking that question, go ahead, make your work. Forget about Mary. But if you really want an audience that matters, chat to the people on the street. Being an arts organisation that is an asset to an area requires listening. Not just asking what is needed here but paying attention. It means consistently inviting the wider community voice into the space, and this takes time and patience. It requires an investment in a process that really asks and really listens and really hears.

A lot can come from a conversation. Our ideas come from conversations we have with people at home, with neighbours or on the street, going to the shop. The stories are already there. They rise to the surface of a conversation and create a sense of curiosity or interest, or a gut feeling that you sense would be good to follow. Something feels important, urgent, exciting.

Each conversation lays down seeds to get audiences on board. Whether it's properly interviewing people or chatting in the pub, you're creating an energy around what is about to happen. We work hard to get audiences to see shows, building close relationships with partners, from housing associations to campaigning and voluntary groups. We open doors, invite people in and are genuinely interested and happy to meet people. Conversations early in the process can be about discovering what kind of exchange between a show and audience might need to be created. What conversation could happen? How might it land? What can it do to influence change?

Conversations can be difficult. People make prejudiced comments and we have to challenge them. Life can be shitty and hard, and people can express that through divisive views on issues and demeaning opinions about each other. It's a matter of listening to views that contrast with our own and making clear decisions in response. The decision could be to challenge and walk away. It could also be to stay and carry on talking, as the things people are saying suggest that we need more complexity in a show. Often, it's a bit of all of this. It's about sidelining hate and despair while representing complexity and telling a version of the story that builds a movement for change.

Regardless of the challenges, put the effort in, get out and talk to people. Especially people who might never go to a show like yours. Let them know it will be a good night out, fun, stimulating and interesting. And then make it a good night out! Make a show that allows your audience to relax, that doesn't judge them if they get their phone out or eat a bag of crisps or a burger. Make a show that's robust enough for people to enjoy. Theatre is entertainment. Keep the tickets cheap. Even better, give them away.

## Pay attention

Keep your radar up – what's interesting? What's going on? What's the thing that feels urgent? What's the thing that nobody's talking about but everyone knows is happening? What's the thing that keeps coming up in conversations, that feels like it could change? The thing that is right on the edge? Who are the people doing the interesting things and who might be misunderstood, who you want to get to know? What have they got to say? What's happening that speaks to you and will also speak to someone over there? Keep your radar up in the rehearsal room. Someone just said something genius – great, bottle it. Something just felt really strange and incredibly moving – why? Pay attention to all these moments. They're going to help you make something powerful.

Make friends, listen well, bring people in, bring people together, create space to dream – and to eat. Make it nice, offer resources, tea and coffee, a place to work, access to a printer. Go for walks, go to the theatre, get artists to come to you. Work with your friends, work with people you don't know, work with people who hate theatre. Make shows in houses, in parks, on bikes, in the cities. Protest, see protest as art, see protest as theatre. There are no stupid questions, make mistakes, fail, be brave.

Pay attention to the industry. Know that theatres and galleries and arts centres are public spaces that belong to you. If you're in the UK (or a similarly privileged country), know that the arts council and your local council are publicly funded, paid for by the National Lottery and taxes, and you can use them as a resource. Speak to the council officers, ask for support, ask for advice. Invite people who work in theatres to your shows – show them what you're made of. Don't be afraid of them.

A quick aside: for a long time, we didn't receive any funding at all. We never even tried. We were intimidated by the thought of all those people in suits judging us – it wasn't our world. Us with the wrong accents and no connections. It turned out that our first contact at the arts council was a bit of a scruff with wild hair like a Fraggle. We couldn't believe it. His name, when it arrived on our letters, had been a massive statement of authority and we were too scared to ring him for a year. It seems mad now, but when you've grown up in a world where 'council officer' means unwelcome interference in your family and community, it's hard to not be nervous.

To pay attention is to stay curious and hopeful, and that is political. So much of life is crappy – we want to look away, shut our eyes, put our heads in the sand, hide under the covers. Climate doom, toxic politics, the far right, inequality, the immorality of the corporate sector and so on. And so on. It can be easier to connect to the familiar and comforting, than to really open our eyes, turn on our senses and tune in to the world. It's difficult to find places to look, with nerve endings open, without getting burned. But if you pay attention, there's always another possibility – another future that is and was possible – in the things that are happening and the things that have happened, however hard they are. The same goes for historical injustice. It didn't just happen. In every moment of every day, there are things being said, thought, felt and imagined that open up or shut out possible worlds.

## Circular process

We think of our work as a circular process. The phrase describes how we begin, what we do, how it grows, how it feeds itself, how it keeps transforming. How things build inside each show and from show to show. Someone we spoke to once becomes part of a show five years down the line. We start by talking to people, building the picture with people who are left wing, right wing – the protagonists, the bystanders, their friends, their enemies. We hold workshops. We gather our gang and we research, experiment, make, produce. The ripples create the next set of opportunities.

Circular process is a way of thinking about how we join in with what is already there. Not coming in with a heavy hammer, breaking something down, building something temporary and leaving. Transformation is circular, not linear. So often in work that is close to communities like ours, there's an expectation that the show happens, the people are empowered, they improve in confidence and resilience. They get a job, buy more stuff, grow the economy. We're not about that. We don't measure value like that. We don't have a 'theory of change'. There is no transformation outside of being here, saying yes and seeing what happens next. Joining in. Circular process is a way of thinking about how to be accountable. And it doesn't mean being countable. There is no population to be fixed in time and place, just lots of movement – improvisation, experience, doing it yourself, having a go, making something out of nothing, saying something new, seeing what happens next.

## Co-creation – what's that word about?

Our process is collaborative. Everybody's ideas count and get listened to, and we have all kinds of people in the room when we're making work. If there are experienced professionals in the room, they get listened to on an equal level with people making the show, and to the sister or friend who just dropped in and ended up watching a scene. It's about creating warmth and trust in the room so that people know they can contribute, that their feelings and opinions are wanted and appreciated. It is a very fluid process of giving and taking and listening. Someone comes into rehearsals and says 'I don't get it', and we have a rethink, try something different. We work with an openness where everyone's invited. We all have something to bring, a role to play, and the roles are open. You might be the producer, but you'll have something to say about the work being created by the choreographer. Maybe you can also help paint a wall.

Currently, in the UK, 'co-creation' has become a major buzzword in the arts and cultural sector, and many artists are using it to challenge power imbalances in art-making and institutional decision-making. There is some good work being done. We're on board with challenging power structures, but we find the word 'co-creation' contentious and, at times, a bit of a sham. The roots of co-creation are in the world of 1990s business, where reaching out to 'stakeholders' to co-create new products that appeal to the market makes lots of sense. It's also a difficult term for us because 'true' co-creation is easy to say, but hard to do. Not only that, but we've been in activist circles where we've experimented with consensus decision-making, and it's not so simple. There's usually someone driving the process, and actually that's not always a bad thing, especially when you're working to a timeline and need to get things done.

We're committed to 'cultural democracy' – an idea of art as something that can and should be made with, by and for everyone. Co-creation can be a useful tool sometimes, but it will only ever be one of the tools. While we work collaboratively, we generally don't do 'pure' co-creation in practice. We're not afraid to take the lead and say, this is a good idea, this needs to be made now, let's do it.

## Difficulties – let's be honest

We've said lots of idealistic stuff so far, but it's important to acknowledge that working outside of the safety of a theatre building or gallery, and with people and in places that have been massively underserved, can be hard. The challenges can come thick and fast. That's why you need your gang – a collective of people that you trust, on board with the common why, who understand the contexts you're working in and share your politics.

Here are some the challenges we've had to deal with:

- A performer going out and taking drugs after opening night, getting fucked up, then feeling too ashamed and hungover to come in the next evening. One of the production team had to go to his house and get him out of bed, driving back with car windows wide open to sort him out. He arrived at 7.25pm for a 7.30pm show stinking of booze and really upset the rest of the cast. We learned to really talk to casts about the highs and lows of a show and about respecting the whole team.
- A performer receiving a court date at a pivotal time, threatening production schedules and tour plans. Ultimately, there are systems beyond our control that we can't change. We try to work flexibly and know it's not the end of the world if someone doesn't make it to a dress rehearsal. We have a Plan A, Plan B, and try to not be too precious about the 'art'.

- A performer who was rather anti-authority being talked down to by a condescending stage manager, creating arguments. We've learned to check production and creative teams in advance for how experienced they are in working with people new to theatre and how flexible they can be.
- Working in places where there has been human shit to clean up. That's no one's job, but ultimately someone will need to do it. Make sure you appreciate the person who does.
- Someone being openly racist. We've had to challenge that right away to safeguard people, but we've also needed to do this in a way that doesn't exclude and that tries to understand where those views are coming from.

These kinds of challenges arise from specific situations and they require an ability to work collectively and sensitively, as well as improvise the best response possible within what are sometimes a limited range of options. Often the challenges relate to something that we get asked about a lot – what kinds of pastoral care do you need when working with people new to performing? (See 'How to take care' in 'Making'.) But there are also other kinds of challenges that have led to important learning for us, and are worth noting here:

- **Casting** can happen easily, with people becoming part of the cast of shows through conversations and relationships that happen organically. But sometimes casting can be really hard and time-consuming, and we've learned to give space over to getting it right. You write in the callout 'We're looking for people with experience of cleaning', and you'll get professional actors who've done a summer cleaning job with very little experience of cleaning for a living. It's important to strike the right balance between being open and being specific in your call.
- **Press** can lead to promotional images getting bad attention and online trolls misconstruing what you are trying to do. We've learned to be mindful at every stage of putting out information about the show, as negative judgements

can harm performers. On one occasion, someone we were working with got interviewed by the *Telegraph*, and the *Daily Mail* picked up the story and gave it a sensational headline. We realised how careful we need to be talking to ANY press and that media training for the company and cast is important.
- **Partnerships** are vital, but finding partners that share our values is challenging. We've started working together, thinking we're all on the same page, but then ended up in situations where partners make a decision that shows they don't take working class people seriously or know how to engage with them respectfully. We've also partnered with activists and our partner involvement has been misconstrued. This has led to us being threatened with funding cuts and we've had to explain and defend our decisions. It's better to think ahead and have conversations to inform key partners, including funders, early on, so nobody gets caught out.
- **Communications** keep everything ticking along, but we've not always communicated well, internally. Keeping people informed, up to date, sharing decisions and how you came to them, and making time for everyone to digest those things is really important. Working with strong producers has helped with this.

2 *Radical Acts*, Bradford, 2018. Credit: Lizzie Coombes

3 *In Common*, Bradford, 2024. Credit: Pishdaad Modaressi

# SITES, GHOSTS, TRANSFORMATIONS

***Read on for:*** *the show starts before you get there; ghosts; touring and being responsive; layering; building on what's already there | building with people; sites–ghosts–transformations*

Site-specific performance takes you out of arts spaces and closer to where people live and work. We wanted to make theatre for the communities we're from and who rarely have an opportunity to see experimental work. We're often working in spaces that have not been used for years, from empty shop fronts to neglected rooms at the back of clubs. The work is about breathing life into buildings but also into people, including ourselves and the artists we work with.

The sites we find for our shows tend to be in areas where theatre buildings don't exist. We start from scratch, building our own infrastructure to create spaces where people can gather.

In Cardiff, we imagine theatre into every nook and cranny of our neighbourhoods in the east of the city, transforming derelict walls into exhibition sites, a school into an arts centre and a community centre into a nightclub. In Bradford, as well as performances made in boxing gyms, car parks, residential houses, youth and community centres and City Hall, we've transformed an abandoned youth opportunity centre into a space designed by young people – a living environment reminding them to be radical and dream big.

The process we use to make a show tends to start with and be shaped by a building. We look for sites that amplify meaning and power and provide lots of opportunities to create feelings and worlds. Sites are playgrounds to build on, helping to structure an audience journey by offering spaces that orientate and disorientate. In sites you find layers that inspire responses, from that beautiful corner with its coatings of paint to that leaky bit of roof that's left a pattern on the walls. Making theatre is about making images, moments, movement, fragments of story. Buildings and other found spaces offer invitations to make.

The site informs what we do – we respond to its architecture, its history and politics – to what's happened there before. So often there's no need to make anything up. It already exists, in the fabric of the building, in the surrounding landscape and in the stories that people tell.

We don't need studio time – we just need a good site to start working in. Working outside of theatres means we don't need to spend energy navigating institutional processes or wait for cultural gatekeepers to give us permission. We've been able to be more self-sufficient.

Site-specific work isn't straightforward. We have to lead on getting everything in place, creating all the inner workings of what makes a show happen from scratch: we set up the front of house, make sure it's safe, think about how it's accessible to people – it's all down to us. This can sometimes be costly, but it's also liberating, because we get to do it how we like and challenge some of the stuffy ways in which theatres often operate.

Theatre buildings come with codes of behaviour that can exclude people right from the start. The spaces we make work in are not forbidding or inaccessible. They are where working class people already go and feel comfortable. We are wary of end-on staging typical of mainstream theatre, with audiences trapped in the dark, trying not to make any noise. Our staging is very open, audiences are close to the action, and we encourage them to look and move around, making their own pictures. So much of life can involve navigating places where you feel you don't belong. For us, working site-specifically is about creating utopian spaces where people are free to be themselves.

## The show starts before you get there

You discover the show from being on site. From the conversations you have with kids on the street, men in the social club, and as part of the interviews you've done. Some of that local knowledge might shift the big idea behind the show and some might find its way into the show. Many shows are possible, more than you can possibly find in the time you have. Countless shows not witnessed by anyone, stories hidden round corners, waiting quietly for the next person.

There's something about the layers of history in a site. Many people have stood where you stand, conversations of all kinds have happened. As a maker, you animate the site with life and action. There is often defiance in how we animate a site, so that it also becomes a reclaiming of that site. Confronting the historical trauma associated with it, for example – an ancient wood where a murder happened, a site of a bombing and death of innocent people, a knocked-down community centre. Our exploration of sites is poetic and political, inspired by the site's history, the surrounding community, the feelings we have in that place and its architecture, and the human and non-human qualities of a site.

The site shares things with you – it informs and guides you. The walls speak. They hold relevant information. What does this space – a dilapidated warehouse, a library, a car park looking over the whole city – say?

## Ghosts

Each site has power. Each site has ghosts. Sociologist Avery Gordon writes:

> it seemed to me that haunting was precisely the domain of turmoil and trouble, that moment ... when things are not in their assigned places, when the cracks and rigging are exposed, when the people who are meant to be invisible show up without any sign of leaving, when disturbed feelings cannot be put away, when something else, something different from before, seems like it must be done.[5]

---

[5] Avery F. Gordon, *Ghostly Matters: Haunting and the Sociological Imagination*, 2nd edn (Minneapolis, MN, and London: University of Minnesota Press, 2008), p. xvi.

Listen to, tend to, dream about, play and commune with ghosts. Sites have many of them. The experiences that have happened before you arrive demand understanding and sensitive holding. Let the borders between a site's ghosts and your ensemble be porous.

Sites are haunted by layers of memory and history. Images, metaphors, stories are triggered by quirks of architecture or landscape, by a turn of phrase in a conversation, or a relationship you uncover when spending time there. Your imagination is a route to accessing these layers. Who lived in this house? Who might have worked here? What experiences have shaped the detail of this space? How did the people who were here journey round this space? Some sites seem to have more ghosts than others and some ghosts make themselves very present. Some ghosts control the narrative that hangs over spaces and the work then becomes about how we flip those stories.

Ghosts are part of the life of this economic system we call capitalism, because it produces so much destruction and waste. When researching for our show *We're Still Here*, we looked into Tata Steel, the multinational steelmaking company based in India that purchased the steelworks in Port Talbot in 2007. We became inspired by Arundhati Roy's book *Capitalism: A Ghost Story*, in which she describes how corporate capitalists, including the Tata Steel group, were laying waste to land, communities and democracy in India. She cites the famous revolutionary Karl Marx, who described capitalism as having 'conjured up such gigantic means of production and of exchange, that it is like the sorcerer who is no longer able to control the powers of the netherworld whom he has called up by his spells'.[6] For Roy, the powers of the netherworld include poor and dispossessed peoples, as well as the lands, rivers, mountains and forests ravaged by massive industrialisation projects in India. Avery Gordon also thinks of ghosts as carrying those very same

---

[6] Karl Marx, cited in Arundhati Roy, *Capitalism: A Ghost Story* (London: Verso, 2014), p. 8.

otherworldly powers: 'follow the ghosts and spells of power in order to tame this sorcerer and conjure otherwise', she says.[7]

Haunting is not just about death and destruction, but about its refusal. A refusal to go quietly. A refusal to be forgotten. In *We're Still Here*, a group of young performers remained unseen throughout the performance, other than during moments when the site came alive with the sounds of their adventure and play. Their ghostly presence represented a threatened future but also created a sense of energy and potential. A lost generation that capitalism had begun to move on from and leave behind, creating a space for something else. The kids were agile and free in the space, refusing to go away, hinting at an alternative future, yet to be written.

We don't own stories or need them to fix or settle. We're not about extracting stories from the poor and playing to middle class audiences. We keep stories in the community, with the people from the place, our main audience. We speak, make, act, witness from a place that sits inside the past, present and future of that place. We're inspired by cultures that have respectful relationships with ancestors and future generations, sitting in a different sense of time than the product-orientated time machine of capitalism. There are so many ghosts and they tell stories about so many possible times. We find a way to converse with ghosts, discovering what their stories share about the alternative futures that reside in history and memory.

We have seen the direct impact of austerity, the economic policy adopted by successive right-wing governments, played out in our communities. Severe cuts to welfare benefits, public services, educational maintenance grants, stretching the fabric of our already stressed-out communities. With austerity, our high streets seemed to change into ghost towns overnight, with more pawn-brokers, gambling outlets and closed shops. It's not easy. We returned to the cities we were from to grow Common/Wealth

---

[7] Gordon, *Ghostly Matters*, p. 28.

as a company. Returning to the place where you grew up means you are literally returning to all your ghosts. Some of them aren't even ghosts – they're still alive!

The ghosts are there every day and their presence can be weighty. Doing our heads in daily. We're working in these places that have got so much baggage. In South Wales, where our East Cardiff base is, there is this historical imagery of the Welsh Valleys and the working men's clubs and the Land of Song and Poetry. Coming home to work in the area you grew up in, there is history. But it is not that history.

## Touring and being responsive

Touring site-specific performance is a bit of an oxymoron. It's supposed to be specific to site, so how can you tour it? But we're not so purist. With *Our Glass House*, we were excited about making work in a council house because you find council houses everywhere. Touring to sites that are common in many neighbourhoods means that it becomes possible to arrive at a new site, get to know it and adapt the show in response pretty quickly.

When we created Common/Wealth, site-specific work felt exciting and experimental, but often out of reach. It didn't happen often, was costly to access and had very short runs. By touring it, we found a way of making experimental work accessible to more people. We believe in the importance of the stories we're telling and experiences we're making, and we want to get them out there. When on tour, the work is still site-specific. It responds to the new site every time. Every time we transfer, we work in the new site we are given, recreating the show in response to its distinctive qualities. Each new site presents opportunities. We explore what the show might mean here, being responsive and allowing time for the show to take a breath, adapt and transform.

*Our Glass House* explored domestic violence and toured across several neighbourhoods, and every new house presented gifts.

We didn't try to make an exact copy of the show each time. We worked with local people to prepare the site, sharing stories through the process, communicating something of the message even before the first performance. We would move into the house we were making the show in, get to know the community, who built the set with us, and meet our audiences face to face. The conversation about domestic abuse started well before the first performance. Knowing how important accents are for people, we cast some roles locally in each site. Creating that familiarity was important – it was part of our invitation to audiences to become witnesses, to consider their own responsibility when confronted with violence like that in their neighbourhoods.

Touring *Peaceophobia*, a show that responds to Islamophobia and is staged in multistorey car parks, we work with Fuel, our co-producer, and other partners to research and connect with local car clubs, young Muslim groups and mosques. They are contacted before we arrive and then we have three days before the show opens where the actors and Speakers Corner co-directors visit mosques and halal food places, delivering workshops to groups. We tap into new communication networks and get people to spread the word locally; sometimes the local kebab shop is our best resource. We don't want the power dynamic of predominantly white arts audiences watching young Muslim South Asian lads on stage. In some places that's unavoidable as there isn't a substantial Muslim audience, so we also engage the local car scene (there's one everywhere). In Norwich, the car park security guard had a son who ran a car club. They ended up organising their own car-meet at our car park with the actors before a show, bringing together lads from very different backgrounds to share their common passion: cars.

*No Guts, No Heart, No Glory*, a show about Muslim female boxers, was very specific to Bradford, but we toured it to boxing gyms around the UK and internationally. The tour became a way of us continuing to develop the show, meeting new people who connected with it. In Perth, Australia, we worked with mainly Indigenous young people in a high school who made a response piece that explored their own feelings of being demonised in the media, and it was shown on Western Australian news. Artistically, we made discoveries in each new boxing gym, very creative places in their own right, with atmospheres designed to inspire athletes and young people. We took some of those adaptations with us. When we worked in a gym in Manchester's Moss Side area, we loved their brilliant sign – 'Respect, Courage, Dignity' – so much that we recreated it as a permanent piece of the set.

## Layering

We use the term 'layering' to describe how sites layer up with reality. The best sites bring a strong identity that can be played with. It's about finding the connections that resonate and bringing them into the world of the play.

*I Have Met the Enemy* was an international show about war and the arms trade, staged in a youth centre that was also used for army recruitment. In one scene, Shatha, a visual artist in Yemen, speaks to us via a digital link-up and asks Mo'min, a Palestinian performer, and Alex, a former soldier from Wales, to build her living room from the set. We learn that her living room, where we had been invited to sit, had been obliterated by an air strike. A very local site in Bradford finds itself part of a global military-industrial complex revealed by international visitors from Wales, Palestine and Yemen. The ground moves beneath our feet, people and places are connected through sharing an experience, new layers of meaning are revealed.

Bringing these layers to life in a youth centre where the army goes to recruit young working class kids for war felt significant. Revealing the international connections of this place where kids play football and go to youth club. We invited the kids in, showing them our high-tech set. They were amazed by the lasers and the metronomes. That it could even be possible to tell a story like that in a place like this and in a way that people would connect with. And they did connect – they know what injustice feels like and they're angry too. We gave them flyers and free tickets to give to their friends and families. The kids watched us working away and making something ambitious here. The site transformed from youth centre to arms fair, to border zone, to rave, to a living room in Yemen.

Some sites allow you to explore layers of meaning that exist across time as well as space. We made *Radical Acts*, a celebration of disobedient actions that women have taken to make change in their lives, with a group of women in the Bradford Club. A private members' club dating back to 1761, it had long provided a space for elite men to come together and do business. The city of Bradford was designed and orchestrated from the club in a building that did not admit women until 1985. With its architecture steeped in masculinity, it symbolised everything that *Radical Acts* was fighting against. The mission was to flip the building and reclaim it for something we are still fighting for. Full equality, the right to decide, safe homes, safe streets. We worked with the building, drawing on its sombre and impressive atmosphere. Exploring how our cast felt to inhabit and be powerful in this space. Replacing the social energy that keeps capitalism intact with women singing and laughing and screaming and sharing stories of individual and collective strength.

When we tour *Peaceophobia* to multistorey car parks, the streets outside seep in. We hear real-life police cars going past, the call to prayer from a nearby mosque. The sights and sounds of the city animate the car park and the show itself, and the show makes new relationships to the real world throughout the performance.

## Building on what's already there | Building with people

It isn't just about us thinking about site, it is thinking about site in relation to who's around and what's there already.

In sites we find people, and their stories and presence become part of the show. In the Bradford Club we found the barmaid, a woman who went out of her way to accommodate us and make sure we had everything we needed. She shared her experience of domestic abuse after watching *Radical Acts*. 'That happened to me', she said. The openness of Peter, the manager, who understood the importance of gathering these women together to tell this story. While we were rehearsing one time, a far-right group was demonstrating outside, one dressed as a medieval crusader. We shouted at them in the street before returning to the warmth of the club. Stuff like this happens all the time. Because you're not in the protected environment of a rehearsal studio, you're close to things happening in the streets and you have to respond.

*The Deal Versus the People* was made in partnership with the Trade Justice Movement as part of their campaign against the Transatlantic Trade Investment Partnership. This proposed trade agreement threatened democratic rights by overriding government regulation of goods and produce. The show was made with a large cast drawn from across Bradford and was performed in the council chamber of Bradford City Hall. Hundreds of people seated in this beautiful chamber – each seat with its own microphone signifying that every voice matters – facing a platform for the speaker and a large table. A table that we danced on. The site triggered questions – who gets to sit here? Who speaks? Who makes decisions? We staged an occupation of the site for three nights in a row. We used nooks and crannies to hide pots and pans, concealing face masks in drawers underneath the microphones, ready for the moment of takeover. We couldn't build in the site but we could make use of every facet of space, layering it with props, bringing everyday people into the here and now of a democratic site. We had a huge pop-up book depicting the history of the people of Bradford who, way back in the 1830s, thought that the price of bread should be set in accordance with the needs of the people rather than profit-seeking elites. We pressed at the limits of representative democracy, reclaiming a space designed for this, and for us.

## Sites–ghosts–transformations

It's our responsibility to attend to the context of a site and to tend to its future. We don't write the news, where you only get a sliver of a story. Even in places where the most horrific things have happened, you can start to tell a different story. Being from the places we now make shows in means we make work from a place of literal knowing. That's why it's so charged. You don't have to be from a place to make work in it, but you do have to find out those important stories. You have to find a way to converse with ghosts.

Once we'd settled back in our home cities, we began to find ways to work in a sustained way. To continue to tour site-specific performance, but to complement that by creating initiatives that had a continuous presence in our places, tending to our political aims to flip the narratives of place and to reclaim spaces for everyday artistry and creativity, and for all the good things that come from that.

In East Cardiff, where Rhiannon grew up, there are only two places for the community to meet and gather: the community centre and the pub. The neighbourhood is too far from town to draw any exciting opportunities and people rarely come to see us or collaborate with us. We are a problem to be solved. Where the poor people live. The people who come are the services, the police and people who think they can save us. Doing site-specific work enables us to create performance spaces across neighbourhoods where there are few natural venues. We've made work in the community centre, the Conservative club (a show about austerity!), in schools and outdoors. Spaces to gather in working class communities are few and far between, especially in areas like ours, built at a time that coincided with the decline of state welfare (remember right-wing prime minister Margaret Thatcher's famous declaration that there is no such thing as society?). In our neighbourhoods in Cardiff, whole swathes of land are owned by Tesco, a huge supermarket chain, and much of the rest is in the hands of private landowners and the

Church. Making site-specific shows in the heart of communities reclaims space and invites us to reimagine what could happen in places like ours. It signals that people here can be artists and dreamers too.

Our first base in Bradford was an empty shop in the city centre. We ran workshops for the Women of the World (WOW) festival from there. After the first WOW festival, we had 10 women volunteers and 10 young girls energised, having had the best time and wanting to do something positive for Bradford. Speakers Corner was born. We started to look for a building to stage events and had a daft, funny realisation that we didn't need to look: we had a building – our little shop. It was small but mighty. We paid very cheap rent and made it into an inspiring gathering space. We got to work programming the space, and any idea that our collective wanted to try out, we did it, sometimes running four events a week. It was a hotbed of creative and political action. We held protests in the public spaces in the city and always had our place to retreat to. The girls arrived in their school uniforms off the bus and spent most days there. This was all without funding and without a dedicated 'worker', just Evie, Saliha and Sasha in the shop, with the girls taking over the space three times a week. We created campaigns and connected globally with young people in Afghanistan, the US, Palestine, Kashmir. Eight years later, Speakers Corner is still going – still theirs, still autonomous, still doing whatever they want.

In 2020 we moved into Common Space, a former youth opportunity centre in the indoor market. Every year we've been there, the council have told us it would be demolished the following year. This has meant we haven't truly settled or invested in infrastructure. But impending demolition also represented an opportunity: if the building is to be knocked down then we can do something transformative in it. We recreated the building as a space of artistic potential and freedom, and we like the symbolism of transforming what opportunities might look like in our context. We've been those young people who, when they go along, find that there are no opportunities in the opportunity centre. We created *Off the Curriculum*, which featured 16 installations designed by young people, giving a tantalising glimpse of what an education curriculum made by and for young people might offer (see 'Works').

Young people meet in Common Space most nights, for our Youth Theatre Lab, Speakers Corner or to work in the music studio with our friends who use the space, All Star. They come to take a breath and imagine a different world. As one of our Youth Theatre Lab members said:

> When I first saw the building, I already knew there was something fun inside because when you look at the sign, 'Common Space', 'common' means it's caring, it's like your home and you will feel comfortable around the people you're talking to.

The young people are there for hours, in this mad environment, surrounded by remnants of all the events they helped create – we don't get rid of the thing from before and we've built up layers of art on the walls. The space is very clearly theirs. The building is freezing and falling to bits and no one is going to fix it, but we have had the freedom to write all over the walls, make collages and murals, create installations. Anyone new feels the relaxedness. It's not a formal space like a school or a sterile building like an arts venue where the message is 'don't worry, you just don't understand it because you're not a real artist'. Common Space is really gettable from the first minute. It's full of life. It's haunted, in a positive sense, by the young people who have been here before and by what they have made.

4 *Our Glass House*, Bristol, 2012. Credit: Adam Ryzman

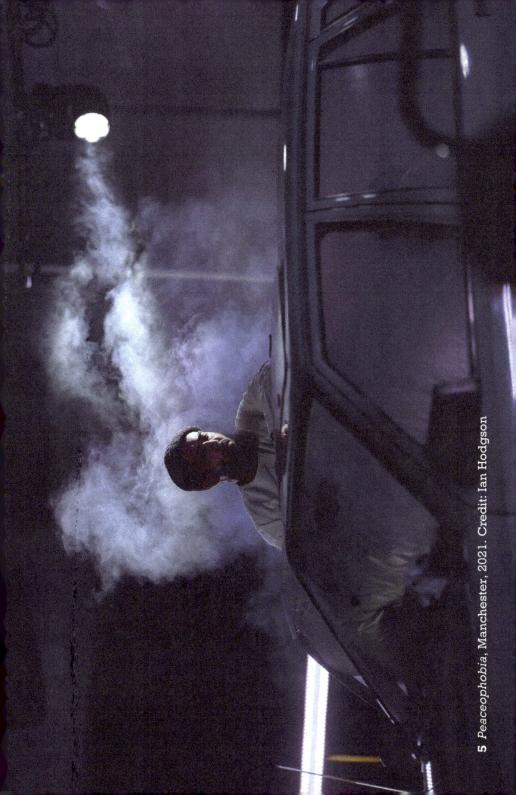

5 *Peaceophobia*, Manchester, 2021. Credit: Ian Hodgson

6. *We're Still Here* Port Talbot 2017 Credit: Ian Pountney

7  *I Have Met the Enemy*, Bradford, 2019. Credit: Karol Wyszynski

8 *I Have Met the Enemy*, Bradford, 2019. Credit: Christopher Nunn

***Read on for:*** *a toolbox for making theatre from scratch, including*

- descriptions of practical exercises,
- reflective pieces on working processes.

We have selected the practical exercises that we find most useful for generating new ideas, bringing people together, playing and experimenting, and building new shows. The reflective pieces written by ourselves and company members respond to questions we are frequently asked relating to our practice. In addition, we invited collaborators to share guidance on their area of skill – set design, lighting, composition, writing political theatre, site-specific performance and other things. Contributions from company members, friends and collaborators start with brief biographical information about the writer. The pieces without a specific author listed were written by one or some combination of the co-authors – Evie, Rhiannon and Jenny. You'll find these in the first half of the section, followed by the pieces written by company members, friends and collaborators.

There is always more than one way of doing things, and most of the exercises here have several different versions. We invite you to take what is useful, skip what isn't, try things out, do it differently next time. Do it yourself, in your own way.

# QUESTIONS TO ASK YOURSELF AT THE START OF MAKING

Why are you making it?

What do you want to say?

Who is the audience?

What form should it take?

What site holds the world?

What change do you want to make?

What do you want to see?

Why are you and your gang the people to make it? What do you bring?

Who do you need in the room as makers?

Who do you need to talk to?

# HOW TO START A PROCESS

Get to know who is in the room, and the stories, histories and contexts of the site you are working in. Create space and time for people to tell their own stories. Think about how to make the space really comfortable for everyone.

We have some go-to exercises that are not too overwhelming for people working in a creative space for the first time, and that unlock ideas and help everyone get to know each other.

## Portraits

Pair up and draw a portrait of your partner, using your non-dominant writing hand (i.e. if you are right-handed, use your left). Draw each other in detail and gift each other the artwork. You can also tell your partner three things about yourself. Each pair shares their portraits with the group and the three things they've learned. Put all the portraits together and make an exhibition of everyone in the room.

This exercise can also be used to create self-portraits.

Drawing with the non-dominant hand gets over any fear of not being able to draw. It usually creates some fun results. People have a laugh at themselves and that can relax everyone straight away. Sometimes we play a song, something that makes people smile and gets them relaxed but that also sets a time limit for the task – the drawing activity lasts just as long as the song.

## The story of your name

In a circle, tell the group your name and the story behind it. Lay out a big piece of paper with lots of coloured pens in the middle of the room. Sit in a circle around the paper and come in one by one to write down your name and share its story. It could be a story of who named you and how, where your name comes from or what it means. It could be a nickname that you have now or that you had as a child. If you don't know or would rather not tell a true story then you can make one up.

Starting with this exercise reassures everyone that they know how to tell stories and there are many stories to tell. Speaking in front of a group can be daunting. This exercise ensures everyone has time to speak and share in a non-scary way. It also provides a good opportunity for people to assert the correct spelling and pronunciation of their name.

## Conversation wheel

The group sits in a circle. Ask the group to pair up, with pairs facing each other.

In pairs, decide who is A and who is B. B will always move.

Set a discussion topic to be chatted about for two minutes.

After two minutes B will move to the next A person along, and sit facing them.

A new discussion topic will be set, and so on ...

This is a useful exercise for opening up a conversation on a topic the group is exploring. The facilitator can set subjects that relate to the topic, with some being more personal and some more to do with the world outside. For example:

- Discussion 1 – chat about your personal experience of voting in an election.
- Discussion 2 – chat about why so many people in the UK choose not to vote.

To make sure both people in the pair get to speak, you could set one-minute timers, with each person taking turns to speak and listen within their pair. We ask people to focus on the qualities of listening and paying attention so everyone is being listened to and the conversations are rich.

## Question and answer

Create a series of open questions or prompts that are brave, personal and fun. You can also do this with themes. Everyone writes three questions or prompts. These could be themed in some way – for example, a personal one, a political one, one about the future. Write them on small bits of paper, fold them up individually and place them in the centre of the circle. Set up the rules:

- Only one person can reach for a piece of paper and read it.
- Only one person can respond.
- If no one wants to respond, sit in silence until someone decides to read the next question/prompt.

Some examples that have worked well for us:

- Tell us about a time you felt judged.
- What do you want the future to look like?
- What is your relationship with the police?

This exercise tends to open up honest, authentic responses which build connection and trust, creating opportunities for people to learn about each other and the experiences and skills in the room. It can also be used to explore the subject matter of your work, giving you insight into personal relationships to the material. The exercise helps a group get used to being vulnerable with each other and encourages people to value experiences equally.

## Being seen and heard

Performing in front of people isn't always easy or comfortable.

Start with the basics. Ask your group: what does it feel like to be seen and to see someone? How do you stand up in front of people and speak? Do you enjoy applause, soaking it up? Or do you feel uncomfortable? How does your body feel? What do you do with your hands!? What do you need when performing? How do you support someone who is performing? A conversation will help you learn from each other's strategies, and know and understand better the journey you need to go on to reach the point of performing in front of each other.

Move on to discuss the focus of your project, what matters about it and what you are trying to achieve. Changing the world or fighting against discrimination? What is it about the topic that is bigger than each of us? This can help feelings shift from anxiety to a shared sense of purpose. What needs to be said? How do we need to do it?

Try these practical exercises:

- In pairs, sit or stand, make eye contact and look at each other. Really see each other. Do this in three rounds. First, sit knee to knee and set a timer for five minutes. Afterwards, chat about it – what did it feel like, to be the one looking and the one looked at? Second round: sit or stand a metre apart and repeat the exercise. Third round: sit or stand two metres apart, and repeat.
- Create a small audience and playing space. One person at a time enters the playing space and stands in front of the audience. They look everyone in the eye. Then they describe how they feel in their body (my feet feel unstable, my heart is racing, etc.), focusing purely on physical description. The

facilitator talks to each part of the body the person has drawn attention to – how would it be if your feet felt rooted? What if your breathing slowed down? The person in front of the audience listens and responds.
- One person enters and stands in front of the audience, looks everyone in the eye and gives them a word. The words can come from a list – a list of family members or a list of vegetables, it doesn't matter. The important thing is to look each person in the eye, give them your word and then move to someone else. Look them in the eye and really gift each person their word. Once each person has completed the task the audience give them a round of applause, and they stay standing and receive it. Each member of the group tries this. Chat afterwards about how this felt.

## What I'm good at/have a dance

Ask everyone in the room to say what their favourite song to dance to is and create a collective playlist. Mark out a dance floor in the space – it can be big or small. Put the music on. Play a version of musical statues – everyone dances, and when the music stops, each person finds another person and tells them what they're good at. This should be something important and personal – for example, 'I'm good at getting my baby brother to sleep', 'I'm good at mediating between my family members', 'I'm good at cooking jerk chicken'. When the music starts up again, everyone continues to dance, then finds a new partner when the music stops and tells them something else they're good at. It has to be something new each time. Chat about how this felt afterwards. Is it hard to share what we're good at? Or do we love it? Feel the energy shift in the room from the dancing and also from the power of sharing what we're good at. This exercise builds hype and energy.

# STAGES OF A DEVISING PROCESS

## Early questions

Why are you making it?

Why are you making it now?

What are you responding to in the world?

What are you exploring?

How do you want the audience to feel?

## Early structure

Make an emotional score (see 'Emotional score' later in this section):

- What emotions are involved?
- What's the journey for the audience?
- How are you going to structure an emotional journey for the audience? (As a guideline only at this stage – it can and will change.)

## Early form: how do you take the audience on that journey?

Think about the things you'd like to see in the show.

What's the world of the play?

What's the potential of this world?

What does it sound like?

What visuals and symbols and gestures define it?

What's the world within? What are the underlying themes, mysteries, ghosts?

Why are the audience there? Who are they? Do they interact, and if so, when and why?

## Research

Gather inspiration: images, music, films, comedy, quotes, sayings.

Speak to people: people with lived experience, friends, family, the community.

Read: articles, poetry, newspapers. Read all around the subject and its themes.

Get into the world: visit places, go to gigs, boxing matches, protests.

## Researching people's experiences

Who do you need to speak to?

Hone your interview questions from the emotional score.

Carry out interviews with as many people as you can who have a relationship to the subject.

Transcribe the interviews: what new themes emerge?

## Casting

As they say, 90% of directing is casting.

Meet with people one to one so they can ask questions.

Keep auditions workshop-style so it's relaxed and not too pressured and you can meet people as they are.

Think about the environment of the audition. How intimidating is it? How many people are in the room? How will you welcome people into the space?

Take photos and make notes (discreetly!) so you can remember.

## Site

Where would be a resonant place to stage the show?

Come up with a list of sites with connections to the work.

Think about where it's important for this show to happen.

Go for walks/cycles/drives in the area you'd like to make the show.

Research who owns any buildings you're interested in and get in touch with them.

## Meet with the team

Choose your team carefully. Listen, read, look at their work. Talk to people who've worked with them. Think about the team dynamic – what do they need to thrive and make their best work.

Meet with the designer, sound composer, lighting designer, writer. Share images, music, reference points. Let ideas stay loose at the beginning.

Keep in regular contact, updating everyone on any significant progress.

Start a shared digital platform or group to share inspiration and ideas from the start.

## R&D

A time of play. Use it to explore lots of avenues with no pressure. Use it as an opportunity to dream big.

Enter R&D prepared and feeling in the world as much as possible.

Plan, plan, plan, even if the plan changes (be flexible and confident about deviating from the plan).

Create exercises to explore and generate material.

Ask, what are the visual moments we want to create?

Write briefs for each section of the emotional journey, so you have some guidelines for what to test and explore.

Have your radar up the whole time. The unexpected things that emerge are usually most interesting.

Build confidence and trust in performers so that they feel willing to open up and to try things outside their comfort zones.

Keep asking, what's the world within?

A lot will get thrown away and that's okay.

Voice-record all improvisations, as some things will be gold.

Document as much as possible – film, write, draw.

As material emerges, start to build the script, however rough.

When time has passed, revisit what happened in the R&D. Hold onto bits, build from and with them, let things go.

## Rehearsals

Keep all the research present in the room so it's easy to refer to.

Create a gallery of images and a playlist of tunes.

Work on site as much as possible. Respond to staging within the space and take everything it has to offer.

Make it nice for people – collectively decide on the structure of working for the day, have drinks and snacks.

Keep exploring structure, and keep a focus on the audience journey.

Go deeper – keep digging – what's it really about?

Get the script down as early as possible so performers can get confident with it.

Use rehearsals to build confidence and performance skills.

If you have actors who are not experienced in performing and playing themselves, be aware of difficult and sensitive moments. Make sure you work on those. Keep building confidence.

Leave plenty of time for technical rehearsal, bringing in design elements – light, sound, video – and experimenting with the cast.

## Shows

Enjoy and celebrate this big moment as a gang. This is what it's all been leading towards. Buy cards, bring flowers, wish everyone luck – it's a big deal.

Make sure everyone comes prepared, feeling good and everything is clear – props are where they are needed, dressing rooms prepared, performers ready.

If you're working site-specifically you might need to set up your own box office/front of house. Ask your friends, or people you trust to be welcoming and set the tone from the start.

Look after everyone.

Keep the energy up. Doing a run is difficult, and sharing yourself every night is exposing. What do people need to keep going?

Think about when performers meet the audience – straight after the show, or do they need a break?

Don't blur the line between the personal and professional – it will be harder for performers to take notes and direction.

What do you want to know from your audiences afterwards? Collect and gather information that will be useful to take things forward. Have chats, collect feedback, make connections.

## Evaluation

How was the journey for you?

What worked and didn't work?

Did we achieve our original aims?

What lessons did we learn?

People not used to theatre warm-ups can feel a bit daft shaking around for what feels like no reason. Let the group know that we warm up so we can leave the outside world behind. The aim of a warm-up is to get the group feeling safe, together and focused, and to create a space that feels different to everyday life. Warm-ups are also a space to play.

It can be useful to create a story for the warm-up so you remember the order, and to guide the group through the different exercises. Warm-ups can be done standing, lying, sitting or leaning on a wall. Think and ask – what does the group need today? How can you build or shift the energy in the room?

Here's one example:

1. SHAKE OFF (shake off the outside world, limb by limb; generate some energy and heat)
2. OPEN (stretches to open up the body)
3. ROOTED (play with feet and grounding)
4. POWER (hold a power pose for two minutes)
5. VOICE (connect with the breath and voice exercises)
6. INTENTION (think about intentions for the session)

There are many ways of doing warm-ups! Each member of the group could offer a stretch or you could make up a dance together as a group with everyone contributing one move. You could use the warm-up to play drama games for fun, energy and team-building (you can find plenty of drama games online). You could play a sport-based game like four square.

## Warming up the body

Warm-ups aren't about being the best dancer or athlete; they are about understanding what we have and feeling good in our bodies. You don't have to be a trained expert on the body to lead a warm-up. Become an explorer, curious about how different bodies move, how people can get to know and understand their bodies, what they can do to be more connected to them, use them, enjoy them, feel more powerful in them. Draw on different body practices – ancient, new, silly.

Here's an example of how we lead a body-based warm-up:

Starting from the top of the head to the toes, pay attention to the body, as if you were about to work with it like clay – mould it into a statue or paint a picture of it.

Moving to the face, begin by massaging in slow, circular motions to loosen the muscles around your mouth, eyes and forehead, and underneath your chin where your tongue rests. We hold so much tension in our faces – release some of it. If you find a bit that feels particularly tense, spend time there, rub it, hold it tighter, go with what feels good.

Smile as wide as you can, stretching your mouth from side to side as far as possible. Purse your lips and make them small in the shape of an O. Be playful. Press your lips together in a big kiss, chew gum, count your teeth with your tongue.

Rub your hands together to create warmth through the friction. Once warm, hold the palms of your hands over your closed eyes. Feel the warmth in your eyelids. Breathe deeply. Imagine the warmth of your hands travelling through your head, down through your torso, your legs, into your feet and out through your toes. Take three deep breaths. Enjoy it.

Move your body. Move the neck, shoulders, torso, arms, hands, fingers, chest, solar plexus, hips, legs and feet. Think about the quality of the movement. Move slowly at first but then change pace. What if you tuned in to what the different parts of your body really needed, and went there?

# WAYS TO WORK WITH THE POLITICAL BODY

Connecting to our bodies is a political act. Politics have shaped your body – what you've experienced, where you stand, how you feel, how you react, how you move. Our bodies can be sites where systems land, where injustice, joy and harm are stored and perhaps held onto. We carry histories through generations.

We are inspired by the work of Fragments Theatre in Jenin, Palestine, who, in the context of a hostile and violent occupation, work with their community to tell their stories. The environment they work in creates fear, stress and anxiety. In a workshop collaboration between women from Wales and Palestine called *The Sea is Mine*, we invited each of our communities to share a skill. So much of what was shared was physical, taking place beyond words: how to dance, how to do self-defence, how to speak Patois and – a moment that stays with us – how to heal ourselves. Saja Maray, a participant from Tulkarem in the West Bank, shared with us the strategy of rubbing our hands together to create heat and holding it on our bodies where we feel pain, letting the warmth sink in – an act of resistance and healing, working with what we have literally to hand.

In moments like this, we discover strategies for the political body. The knowledge passes between us, across borders, between friends. What can you learn and what can you share? Here are some approaches we've picked up from friends, artists, educators and other people we've met along the way.

## Approaches to working with the body

Working from what you need:

- Write down in detail how your body feels today. What needs your attention? Do a warm-up that tends to these needs.
- What if everything and anything was allowed? To lay still, to dance like a rock star, to walk in slow motion, to shake off or have your legs resting up against the wall.
- Write first, then move. Dance for 5 minutes or 50 – it's up to you.

Getting into your body:

- In pairs, one partner lies on the floor, letting their body sink into the ground. The other works with their partner's hands, wrists, arms, feet, ankles, legs – gently lifting, holding and supporting different body parts, exploring how they move.
- Hold your partner's head in both hands, lift it off the ground and support it gently. Feel the weight of it. Slowly move the head from side to side. Take your time, enjoy feeling the mechanics of the body.
- Massage the neck, paying attention to tension points. Keep checking in with your partner and asking what feels good.
- Move down to the arms. Pick up each arm in turn; they should be a dead weight in your hand. Support your partner; lift the arm and explore the mechanics. How do the elbow and shoulders work? What about the wrists? Explore movement and massage the arm at the same time.
- Move on to the hand and the fingers. Notice the details of the hand. Give the arm a little pull and stretch it out. Swap over to the other arm.
- Repeat on the legs, explore how they move, and check how the hip, knee and ankle joints work. Can you lift your partner's legs? Can you make them feel weightless?
- When you finish exploring your partner's body, apply gentle pressure on each body part you've worked on – hold it for a few seconds. Switch over so everyone who wants to gets a go.

## Ways to play and explore the body

- **Lead a journey:** In pairs, go on a journey around the space. You can lead the journey with your eyes closed or open. What happens if one person takes control and then hands over control? How is control shared, distributed? What does it mean to relinquish control? What if you move by yourself? What does it feel like to move without being led, trusting your partner is nearby, taking care of you? Play with the quality of touch, speed, height, depth, architecture and space. Do it indoors or outdoors.
- **Play with weight:** In pairs, in groups, with objects, as a task. What does it mean to hold something heavy, an object, a person? Can you move them? Can you adapt to the challenge? How does it work within a space? What strategy do you need? How do you play with lightness – moving a small object, a feather, a balloon? Or a person, a chair or something heavier?
- **Layering tasks:** Introduce a movement on top of a movement, on top of a practical task. Can you move an object, tell us a story, while changing what you are wearing? Or what if you move the body into a restrictive space, like a cupboard? Or, if you are in a large room, to the centre of the space? Play with the composition of the image you're trying to make. What does it do if it's restricted, or repeated, or in a wide-open space? Do it in the corridors. Use the walls, floor; find places you can balance, rest, hide.
- **Dancing from a memory:** What does it mean to trace the memory of a movement? What if you were to dance the memory of a dance you once did, or just did in an exercise? What if you created from the memory of a feeling, or a time when ..., or the memory of your favourite dance from a music video? Relive, retrace and let the memory lead what it could be and become.

# HOW TO MAKE A RADICAL ACT

We devised this exercise when working on *Radical Acts* (see 'Works'). It's a useful way to find out what's important to people in the room and get them thinking about creative interventions. It gets a group to think practically and inventively about how to engage the public in an idea and need for change. Just as it did for us, this exercise might lead to you doing some radical acts or it might create seeds for your next shows.

**NEED** (5 minutes)

- After moving as a group, stop and close your eyes, hold your belly and your heart, tuning into the two biggest life-giving forces in your body – your breath and your heartbeat. Think about what needs to change in the world around you. The invitation is for you to think of a personal need or something that is close to you or your community. Something that needs to be addressed or needs to be challenged or changed. This will be shared, so think of something you feel comfortable sharing. You don't have long, so think quickly but carefully. What do you or your community need? What's pressing for you right now? Open your eyes and walk to the person opposite you and, for two minutes, share the need you are thinking of. Make sure both of you share.

**MEET** (10 minutes)

- Join another pair and form groups of four. Each person takes it in turn to give a headline of what their need is – for example, 'We need to speak about mental health more'; 'I need to change my housing situation'. As a group, listen to each person's need and choose a need that resonates with you all. This will be the need you'll address. It doesn't mean the other needs are less important or significant, just that this need feels right to address right now, at this moment, for the group.

**ACT** (20 minutes)

- In your group, work on a creative public outcome to the need that you are exploring. This could be ANYTHING. The important thing is that it's creative. You could call it a creative radical act, a creative direct action or an intervention. Something that an audience can witness, anywhere in any way. It's up to you. Think of drawing on the creative skills you have in the group and think of where it should happen (a playground, a bench, outside the town hall). Try to create an idea that will capture public imagination and perhaps have a bit of spectacle about it. What would get people to notice the act? How could you frame it for the public? What does it say to people?

**PERFORM BACK** (5 minutes)

- Each group shares their creative response. This should be performed, not described. You can explain more after you've demonstrated it. It's important to try and find a way to perform it if you can, so you begin to feel it could be real and achievable, and to move towards testing it out.

# TRANSFORM THE SPACE

The facilitator leaves the room, sets a timer, giving the group two minutes to transform the space using objects and furniture in the room. The task is to make the room look completely different. The facilitator counts down from outside the room ('You have one minute left … 30 seconds left'). After two minutes the facilitator enters and the group discusses what they have created.

You can ask the group to transform the space and see what they come up with, or you can give them a theme (e.g. justice). Try not to make the theme a place (e.g. a school) as this tends to make the transformation very literal.

Once the space is transformed, ask the group to:

- Find a place in the room to feel powerful.
- Find a place in the room to hide.
- Find a place in the room that's really comfortable.
- Find a place in the room that's a stage.

If the group has created some writing, you could ask them to choose one of these four positions to share back their written work. This often works if the group has had the same writing prompt. One version of this is that the group share back collectively, speaking one line at a time from different places within the room, with no one deciding who speaks next. This tends to make the group really tune in to each other's writing, sharing lines when it intuitively feels right, to complement or create a sense of tension or opposition.

This exercise transforms rehearsal spaces into more performative places, with a set and a 'stage'. This is really useful for teenagers or rebellious spirits, who might otherwise be disengaged, because it gives them permission to make a mess. The facilitator leaving the room for even two minutes creates a feeling of freedom. The exercise tends to change the energy of a workshop very quickly.

## Follow-up thought exercise

Get the group to consider how they could transform the space with:

- A multiple of one thing.
- With light.
- With a million pounds.
- With sensations – temperature, elements, things they can feel.

# BODY MAPPING

This exercise can be useful for developing character and getting performers to embody characters. Common/Wealth don't necessarily work with 'characters', although it can be useful for performers to create a version of themselves, as if they were in a parallel universe. For example, Mariam Rashid's character in *No Guts, No Heart, No Glory* (see 'Works') was based on a girl her age who wasn't allowed to go to university. We would never ask someone to perform as themselves if this had been their experience - Mariam herself had been to university.

## Step 1

- Draw around a performer's body on big lining paper or equivalent.
- Find a place on the body where the statement 'I fear I am ...' would live. As a group, discuss what that fear is for the character and where it lives – in the hands, legs, etc.?
- Find a place on the body for the statement 'I want to be ...'. Again, discuss where this lives on the body.
- Now create a 'shame event' for the character. Something that happened to them that they have been ashamed of ever since. Find a place for this to live on the body.
- Find places on the body that are more expressive (although please note, if everything is buried in the organs, stomach, heart, brain, the next stages become a little difficult!).

You can do this for each character in turn. The whole group takes part in the discussion, but let the final decisions sit with the performer who will be playing the character. This part of the process takes time – allow 30 minutes for each character.

## Step 2

- The performers walk around the space, focusing on their bodies.
- Based on Step 1, ask the performers to physicalise 'I fear I am ...'.
- Then 'I want to be ...'.
- Then the shame event.
- Ask the performers to try walking with all three present at once.
- Play through a scale of 1 to 10, with 1 being very internal and 10 being very externally physicalised.
- If you want, you can introduce a scenario – for example, you are waiting for an important phone call, you have to leave the house, you are late, you get there and have to wait. Ask the performers to move through the scenario while being aware of the three locations on the body.
- Ask the characters to meet each other and see what happens.

The improvisation is guided by a facilitator who can explore what feels interesting. Allow time for performers to play with the feelings and experiences that come up. Working with music can be helpful.

## Step 3

Afterwards, discuss what you found out about the characters. How will this inform the piece going forwards? What is useful to keep – a shiver on the neck, a gesture of the hands? What can be thrown away?

# WORKING WITH MODES OF ADDRESS

Different modes of address can be fun to try out as ends in themselves or used to develop new material, characters or scenarios. Try the following set-ups:

- Q&A panel discussion – after an improvisation, someone chairs a panel discussion about what happened.
- Post-match interview – after a scene, share feelings about how it went in the style of a football commentator interviewing players after a match.
- On-the-spot interviews – interview a character or a participant about an activity or event as they go about doing it ('I see you are setting up your decks – how did you first get into DJing?').
- Press conference – after an improvisation, stage a press conference. Create a row of journalists to ask questions of the performers ('How do you feel when you box?').

# MAKING UP GAMES | GENERATING IMAGES FROM DISCUSSION

Research a defined subject, then feed the research back to the group and discuss it. Take notes in different colours of:

- Facts and learning.
- Questions we still have.
- Images and concepts that come to mind.

As a group, discuss the whole subject and hone in on an image or concept that feels most interesting to explore right now.

Tell the group that they are to invent a new game, and that their game has to create an expression of the image or concept. Give the group a different instruction to use to create their game. Instructions can include:

- Only use non-verbal sound.
- Only use props.
- You can't touch the floor.
- You can only use touch.

If you have more than one group, make sure the instruction for each group is different.

In one example from our experience, the idea of power led to the concept of 'puppet master on a hill'. The game was as follows:

one member of the group became a puppet master, and they had to get the rest of the group to join them on the hill. Each group member in turn played the puppet master, trying different things to get the group to the hill.

The games can be abstract, literal, comedic or serious. Keep note of all the responses and discuss which concept or image felt the most interesting. The key thing is for everyone to try something and not get too attached to anything. It's not a test for individuals to prove how creative they are. It's about the whole group trying things out.

Inventing games allows you to explore complex ideas by getting everyone on their feet and not too stuck in talking. Physically trying something will prompt more discussion, and games are fun, practical and purposeful ways for the group to explore together. You can spend a whole day like this – research a new subject, chat, invent a game or task, discuss and repeat!

# SIMULTANEOUS CARDS

In pairs, sit or stand opposite each other. You should each have 12 cards. The numbers and pictures on the cards don't mean anything. Take a moment to think of a list of things in your head – childhood memories, favourite places to relax, for example. Turn over your cards at the exact same time as your partner, in complete silence while looking at each other. Then both say one thing from your lists out loud at the same time, turning a new card with each new item on your list. The 'list' can be made up on the spot – it's better when things aren't pre-planned, as you might discover things from listening to your partner.

This exercise is about getting in tune with each other and allowing other people's thoughts and memories to spark off your own. Everyone is leaning in. The words have a choral effect and the pauses, when they come, create space for meaning to circulate. It can be really powerful to watch.

You can start the exercise with people close to each other and then create more distance as the exercise progresses.

We developed this exercise for *Our Glass House* (see 'Works'). In that show, each character was in a different room. They all had to listen in, turning their cards at the same time while listing the times their partners had controlled them (the show was about domestic violence). The challenge was to do the task simultaneously. No one could lead it – and because they couldn't see each other, they had to listen acutely. Sometimes it took five minutes to speak their incidents. The atmosphere was intense – you could hear a pin drop.

# TASKS AS PROMPTS FOR DEVISING

Here are a few prompts we've used across the years. The tasks can be used as a starting point, or as something to add to an idea or a performance as you experiment and make. We sometimes layer these tasks up with each other, and with text, music and images. You can make up your own prompts with what is available to you in the room or objects relevant to the piece you're working on.

- How do you greet a long-lost friend?
- How do you say goodbye?
- Two people dance, holding an apple between their heads.
- Find three moments of unity.
- Apply a limit to movement – energy at 90%, 70%, 10%.
- Freeze the performers, then sculpt them into different positions and try the scene again.
- Order objects in the room by size, by colour, by shape.
- Create three gestures based on a word. The word could be linked to the content of the show you're making, e.g. love, restriction, power.
- Find different ways to dance – together, alone, small, big, like it's the end of the world.
- Perform a karaoke song.
- Pour a jug of water into a cup from different heights, play with distance.
- Play with the tension of doing something a bit dangerous.
- Walk to all four corners of the room and do something in each.
- Pose for a photograph.
- Use chalk to draw on the walls or on the paths outside.
- Create a megaphone moment for everyone.
- Give advice to someone.

- Play the scene while counting down from 20 in your head or out loud.
- Try and take your fingers off.
- Surprise us.
- Hold onto something.
- Trace the architecture of the building with your body.
- Tidy up.
- Take something apart or put something back together.
- Build something new.
- Make us laugh.
- Tear up a photo and put it back together while sharing text.

Add intention and invention to the scenes that come out of this. So, for example, perform:

- With speed.
- Slowly.
- As if your body is heavy.
- As if you need the toilet.
- As if you are late for a train.
- As if you are tired.
- As if you are not happy to be watched.
- As if being watched is the most important thing to you.
- As if you are thirsty.
- As if the floor is hot.
- As if you were underwater.
- As if you were begging for your life.
- As if you have all the answers.

## Real tasks

Think of the real world of your performers in your chosen site. What tasks can they perform? In *Peaceophobia*, which was inspired by car culture, the performers jack up a car and fit all four tyres, timing with precision when the bolts are fastened to punctuate the text. In *Fast, Fast, Slow*, a show about fast fashion, 15 models walked the catwalk, one at a time, each taking off an item of clothing and tossing it in a pile to make a waste mountain on stage. With *No Guts, No Heart, No Glory*, a show made with young Muslim female boxers, the performers boxed for real while delivering text.

Layer tasks, get someone to move, speak some text and reorganise the room. Get another performer to be in charge of the lighting, how it moves, where it lands, while making sounds into a microphone or changing the music. Enjoy exploring the complex and mundane, alongside the honest and stripped back.

Prompts are useful to get people started with writing and can also be a great stimulus for developing the first draft of a scene.

### Lists

A list of the lies you've been told, a list of slang-words, a list of your favourite things to do.

### A fuck you letter

An angry letter to someone in power, a rant, that can be directed at a specific person (e.g. the prime minister) or at a system or institution (e.g. the police or your school).

### Timelines

Timeline of a day/a week/a year/an incident. This could be minute by minute, hour by hour, day by day, with as much or as little detail as you like.

### Make them up

Make up a prompt to support the focus of the specific project – for example, 'Because we're young, they think ...'.

### Why we're here

Complete the sentences 'I'm here because ...' and 'We're here because ...'.

## Object writing

Bring an object in or find an object in your site. Write from the perspective of that object. It could be about what the object sees or has seen or what the object means to you.

## Poem about place

Write a poem in first person from the perspective of the place you live. Every line begins with 'I am ...'. What does your place feel like? What does it see, smell, hear? How is it treated?

We use this exercise to create nearly every piece of work we make. It's a dramaturgical device that is sometimes really present in a work and at other times more useful early on in the making process, fading away as the show develops. This exercise can be done with the creative team, cast or wider group that you're making the piece with. It's a useful way to get the team on the same page and provide a starting point for devising and making.

- Brainstorm all the emotions to do with your piece and write them down on paper. There can be as many as you want.
- As a group, either through discussion or voting, try to narrow these down to five emotions. We find five emotions are useful for shaping a piece. Each emotion state can last for 10 minutes with a 2-minute transition in between, creating an hour-long piece (our preferred length for any show).
- Encourage the group to choose different emotional states so the piece doesn't end up being one note (e.g. all uplifting, all hopeless).
- Write out your five chosen emotional states on five different pieces of paper.
- Explain to the group that you want the audience to go on a journey and that you want the journey to have a clear shape with highs and lows.
- Position the five emotions in an order and see what feels best. The order doesn't have to align with the journey of the characters in your piece (e.g. something sad happens and someone comes and makes things better). The emotional score works best when it maps the emotional journey you want the AUDIENCE to go on, rather than the character/s.
- Discuss and answer these questions: how do we want the audience to feel at the start of the piece? How do we want them to feel at the end? Do we want the piece to end on a hopeful note or one of frustration?

- Play with the shape by putting emotions in a different order and discussing.
- If you are working with multiple performers that have simultaneous journeys, you can map this out for them across the emotional score. For example, with *Our Glass House*, the emotional score started with 'Love', and this was different for each character. For the teenage girl, love was pole dancing and feeling confident and sexy. For the pregnant woman, it was talking about the time they first met their partner. For the young boy, it was feeling free and drawing and playing in different places around the house.
- Once you have the emotional score, you can use it to devise from. Plan interview questions, choreography and exercises that relate to the emotional score.

## Example emotional scores

*Our Glass House*:

LOVE      FEAR      CONTROL      EXPECTATION      COURAGE

*Peaceophobia*:

PRIDE      PARANOIA      ADRENALINE      FEAR      FREEDOM

# How to work from a political starting point

Map out the politics of a subject as early as possible – this will really help you. Speak to friends, family, people on your street, campaign groups, politicians, activists, lawyers, university lecturers. Place people's experience at the heart of your research. Who has been affected by the issue you're exploring? How can you find out more? Make sure everyone understands what you mean when you say that our lives are political and we all have important things to say.

Visit libraries and sites of interest. People-watch. Walk about, chat to people at bus stops. What do people think of the subject, and your idea for how to approach it? Does it feel relevant and necessary to the people you meet?

## Personal-political timeline

Draw a line on a massive sheet of paper, making sure there is space above and below the line. Write dates on the line drawn from the timeline you want to explore. It could be decades, years, months or weeks. Above the line, write the political timeline that relates to the subject you're exploring: for example, new laws, elections, conflicts, scandals, protests, movements, disasters. Below the line, write significant events from your own life or the group's life. Where relevant, make connections between political and personal events. This is a great exercise to do collectively. It draws on the knowledge of the group and builds understanding.

## Excerpt from *Peaceophobia*

In this section of the show, Ali is trying to share the timeline of the VW Golf. The car has a speaker inside and keeps interrupting with a timeline of political events that Casper and Sohail relate to on a personal level. The scene was developed directly from the personal-political timeline exercise.

**car speaks:** 2001, the Bradford riots

**casper:** think i were about 6

**ali:** no-one asked, back to / the golf[8]

**car speaks:** 9/11

**ali:** for fuck's sake

**sohail:** just remember my mum crying and praying

**ali:** bruv not now

**car speaks:** 2003, the prevent policy introduced

**ali:** satya naas

**car speaks:** 2003, illegal invasion of Iraq

**casper:** went to London demonstrations with dad, coaches of us went down

**ali:** in 2003 the mark 5 gti came out, then later on they brought out an edition 30, it had uprated engine parts which made it quicker than the average 2 litre turbo

**car speaks:** 2005, the London bombings

**sohail:** the next few years friends of family people i know getting arrested on suspicion of terror

**casper:** released or arrested?

---

[8] The spaced slash (' / ') is used to highlight where two characters are speaking at the same time as each other, and the dialogue overlaps.

**sohail:** released, i tried to make light of it, at school i got detention for telling everyone my new dj name

terror

wrist

dj terror wrist

# HOW TO WORK ARTISTICALLY IN A SITE

Spending time in a new site is one of our favourite things to do. Getting to know a site physically and metaphorically can lead to lots of discoveries. If there are people hanging about, chat to them. Get them to show you their favourite spot and to tell you what they know about the place.

Questions to ask yourself about a site:

- What happened here? Who lives here? What lives here?
- What does it mean to make theatre in this place at this time?
- How does this site amplify the politics of the story you want to tell?
- How can we find the stories hidden here?
- Who do we need to speak to?
- How can we create a sense of energy and buzz here?
- Who will we gather and bring in?

Spend time in the site and set yourself tasks. Play games. Try things out:

- Walk aimlessly and get lost.
- Walk alone and notice:
    - Smells.
    - Sounds.
    - At least five words (written or spoken).
    - A pattern (something that repeats in some way).
    - Something political (could be to do with cars, shops, houses, rubbish).
    - Something personal (to you or to someone else).

- Find someone to talk to. Ask them about the place. What do they love about it, what do they hate?
- Tour the site, ask the performers – what stories might this wall hold? This windowsill? This shattered stone?
- Work as a group to make a gallery:
  - Find somewhere to sit quietly and draw what you see.
  - Take photos of interesting sights.
  - Pick up objects from a site.
  - Come back together to make the gallery. Pick an exhibit that isn't yours; on the back of the pictures you've chosen, write three words to describe how that person sees the world.
  - Discuss and share observations.
- Play hide and seek.
- Touch all the walls.
- Cross the space without touching the floor.
- Make yourself or someone else big or small.
- Create as many images as possible. If you move the performer and actor here, or there, what pictures and stories can you discover?
- Rub the texture of the building onto paper with a crayon.
- Sit or lie down in different places – in the centre, a corner, an edge, high up or low down, and repeat the above.
- If there's an open space or a gap that leads somewhere, can you journey through it? How can you do that? Can you create a journey for others?
- Write a declaration for the site. If it could speak, what would it say? What would it say to different people?

# HOW TO FIND A SITE

Shy bairns get nowt. Walk around an area you like, note the interesting looking buildings, pop in and ask. If all else fails, squat the lot!

## Find out who owns it

You can do this by chatting to people who live and work nearby – more often than not, they'll know everything about a place. If in doubt, do a Land Registry search. You have to pay a small amount, but this should give you the information you need.

## Be brave – ask for what you need

If the building can be sourced by the council, local government, housing association or similar, be brave enough to ask them for what you need. Call them up and share your vision and don't hold back. Find what your organisations align on. This can help set up a healthy partnership.

## Go to the places where you least expect to make friends

A gym in the industrial estate, a private members bar, a Conservative club. Find the hidden gems, visit them, make friends with the people who work there. They want good things to happen in the community too and won't be expecting a visit from the likes of you.

## Get close to where people live

Think about the building and its relationship to people. Is it a place people already use? Is it a place where people gather? Find a place that people will find evocative and meaningful. Will they drive past it on the way home and remember the time they saw a show there?

## Trust in the place and people already there

They know the building best, how it works and doesn't work. Who might be the best person to fix it when it breaks, who the people are that use the building and what times they are around. Sometimes, the best way of finding out the history of a site might be the people who hang around it – the lads who smoke weed there, the daytime drinkers who sit at the bar. Ask them, find out and at the same time build your audiences and your advocates.

# HOW TO INTERVIEW PEOPLE

We conduct interviews to inform and shape our pieces. Interviews with the cast, campaigners, community members, workers – whoever has experience of the topic we're addressing. Interviews can take different forms:

- Formal interviews with questions that are the same for everyone, sometimes shaped by the emotional score.
- Interviews tailored to the specific person.
- A guided conversation with a group.
- Exercises to encourage conversation – useful when working with a cast in an R&D setting.

Tips: Keep your voice recorder on, as sometimes it's the chat after the conversation has finished which has the most interesting stuff. Also, with group discussions, keep track of who's said what, so you can go back and gain consent if needed.

It's important that everyone you interview knows that they have the power as an editor to inform the text and change the script. BEFORE the interview, make it clear that:

- People don't have to answer any questions they're not comfortable with.
- If they say something in flow but don't want anyone to hear it later, you will make sure that it is cut.
- The interview transcript and recording will be shared but only with a very small group – usually, just the writer and directors. Let them know who these people are.

- The recording is just for memory purposes and will not be used in the production.
- If their words or story or anything they've referenced is used in the show, you will check this with them in advance and send a draft of the script for them to approve, amend or refuse.
- They will be invited to rehearsals to check how their contribution feels in performance and provide feedback.
- If the performers did interviews and are performing from their own interview material – then it's completely okay for them to change the script at any time. We can rehearse alternative lines with them on the day of the show if need be.

We sometimes ask interviewees to sign a consent form, as this formally confirms we have consent to share their words and they understand that their story may become part of a show. You can find samples of consent forms online. Good consent forms describe what is going to happen to the information people give in clear and simple terms, and provide a named contact should they have any questions later on. Even after signing a form, we make it clear that the contributors still have ownership. If they change their mind later, we'll adapt the show accordingly. It is so important to keep clear communication with people every step of the way. Celebrate the wins with them and share the story of the journey of the show.

## Example interview questions – *Our Glass House*

Here are the questions we used to interview survivors of domestic abuse for *Our Glass House*, based on our emotional score (LOVE/FEAR/CONTROL/EXPECTATION/COURAGE). We tend to use the phrase 'can you' to open questions to show respect and give agency to the person we're interviewing. They choose if they can or want to answer that question.

- Can you talk about the first time you met your partner?
- Did you live together? If so, can you describe your home?
- Can you describe a specific room in the house?

- Can you tell us about a time when you felt really in love?
- Were there any warning signs leading up to the abuse?
- Can you remember the first time the abuse happened?
- Can you describe any ways that your partner used technology and social media in a controlling way?
- Can you tell us about the effect it had on your family?
- How did your home feel at that time?
- Can you tell us about how the abuse affected your child or children?
- Is there anyone you talked to about it?
- What was your opinion of yourself at that time?
- Can you describe the day that you left? Did you make plans? What did you take?
- Can you describe the feeling when you got him out of your system?
- Can you tell us some of the music you remember from that time?

# HOW TO WORK FROM PEOPLE'S EXPERIENCES

- When working with new performers to make a piece, shape it so that they can tell their own stories in their own way. Give performers playing themselves complete control over their story and the way it is told.
- Sometimes people need support to believe in the relevance of their experiences – to believe that sharing an experience is going to be powerful and will speak to other people.
- Go for fullness and complexity. So often performances that draw on people's experiences present their trauma. Working class experience sometimes only seems to be legible to middle class theatre-makers when there is trauma! People's quirky, funny, surprising, everyday stories offer so much.
- When people are performing as themselves on stage, you can weave in some protection by creating a 'character'. Invite them to draw on their own experiences and also character traits of people they know or have come across. This can help create some distance if performers want that.
- When using interviews, invite the people you've interviewed into rehearsals where they can be important sense-checkers, curators and editors. They often have great ideas for set, props, lighting and more.
- Sometimes a juicy bit that you love won't end up in the show because someone wants their mum to come and they don't want their mum to hear that bit. And that's totally fine! Don't be too precious.

# HOW TO WORK IN A NEIGHBOURHOOD

Remember: Neighbourhoods are not places to do things to people. The people living there don't need art projects to save them.

Questions to ask yourself before working in a neighbourhood:

- How are you increasing the wealth already there?
- How are you making sure you don't extract without giving something back?
- Who are your neighbours? What do they like? What do they have in common?
- Why are you doing this work?
- What's the idea driving the work?
- Are people living there on board with it?
- How are you being of service here?

Tips for neighbourhood working:

- Share all of your resources. Share all of the opportunities.
- Be open to learning from others.
- Ask the community what they'd like to see, do, experience, be part of.
- Think about the lens you're wearing – you might need to look differently to see what is there.
- Look for the brilliant people making things happen on their own terms without the support of big organisations and with little or no funding. You'll find them if you look. They do it for love and because they know it's important. Work with them if you can – make them your allies. In other words, find the common wealth that is already there and work with it (not against it).

- Create mini-parties wherever you go – bring sweets and drinks, play music, have a laugh, invite the kids to play, have a good time.
- Build networks and make them informal. Support each other to try things, test out ideas, create something new.
- Dip into complex and difficult things when it feels right. Don't be afraid to talk politics. Sit with it. Hold the complexity. You'll encounter some of the most political people you'll ever meet.
- Stretch people. Get them speaking at events and on platforms.
- Build trust by being open and transparent.
- Be excellent. People deserve the best.
- Collaborate with people who give a shit and have the best interests of the community in their hearts – the youth service, coffee morning meeting, university class, school group, environmental charity.
- Produce an artistic programme that people care about and have ownership of.
- When people come to your shows or your events or your projects, make them feel like a million dollars.

# HOW TO TAKE CARE

We're often asked how we take care of the people involved in our shows. People are at the centre of our processes and so, when serious issues come up for cast or crew, we try not to make a song and dance about it – we just carry on being flexible to who we all are and what we all need. We allow that to change in response to the things life can throw at people.

## How we take care

We accept people as they are – we say, please come as you are.

We never lose sight of the person or the people, regardless of how difficult the challenge is.

We trust people to know the situation that they are in, to know what they need and what the best course of action is. Sometimes it's just about supporting them with that.

We know that people are capable of the most inspiring things.

We know that sustained underinvestment has created deep stresses in working class communities, and that these get expressed in different ways.

We create space and time to talk about whatever is coming up.

We don't insist on keeping to schedules. We work around what's coming up in people's lives – changing plans and direction as and when needed.

Some shows take a long time to develop, because that's how long it takes to create the right relationships and to make a show work around the complex stuff that happens in people's lives. Sometimes, because of that, brilliant shows never get made and it is right to let them go.

We appreciate the skills that all the crew bring and involve the performers in this too so there's appreciation for everyone's talent and energy.

We stay in touch with why we're making the show, that it's bigger than all of us.

Sometimes people who have felt class injustice have run away from the place they grew up in for good reasons, and they carry a lot of pain. We hold that carefully, supporting but not smothering people. Often, it's just about being there to listen.

We have chats around these questions: how are we going to work as a group? How is the group dynamic having an impact on all of us, and on the work? How can we nurture each other better, creating an environment that is good to work in and is generative?

We talk about the risks of sharing personal experiences in workshops and performances. It can be exposing and exhausting. We make sure people know that they are in charge of what goes into (and what has to be taken out of) a show.

When people have a free licence to work creatively with their own experience, they can go anywhere, and some of the places they go to might be hard for other people to hear and even cause offence. We talk about the parameters needed around the work and make agreements that protect everyone.

Where people are taking a break from normal commitments to be in our plays, we pay them properly. We implement compassionate and fair working practices (taking breaks, working accessibly, etc.).

People unfamiliar with the freelance world who decide to take a break from their normal lives to be part of the show need support to understand what they are taking on. The choices they have and the consequences of those choices. Before we start, we talk through how they will navigate the return to everyday life once the show is over.

Shows end, people have a downer. They've been on a high and then there's a crash. We plan ahead to keep supporting people after the close community ends.

We keep in touch with people afterwards.

# HOW TO EVALUATE

We use a sequence of questions to evaluate our work. Developed from our values, they are accessible and easy to use. We use them at different points in a process to guide reflection and to make sure we're staying on track with our aims as a company. The questions are phrased in past tense, but they can be used before, at the beginning, middle and end of processes. Below is an example of our questions, but you could – of course – make up your own!

## Short question sequence (useful when you don't have much time)

- Did we engage working class people?
- Did we experiment?
- Was a story told that was important to the people and the place?
- What change did we create and how far did its ripples flow?
- Did we treat everyone well? Who needs appreciating and looking after now?

## Long question sequence (useful when you have more time)

People:

- Did we engage working class people and audiences, or people new to the theatre? Could everyone access the work?
- Who did we collaborate with, and how? How did they have a stake in what happened?
- How did they experience us, and the process?

- Thinking about audiences and collaborators, what common wealth was tapped into, replenished and created by our work?

Form and content:

- Was a story told that was important to the people and the place? Was the story clear and relevant? Did everyone know why it was important?
- How far did the story reach?
- What new forms did we create? How did we experiment? How was the project multidisciplinary?

Change:

- What ripples did we create and how big were these? What shape did they take? Were they local, national, international?
- Did we also change?
- What is the legacy of all this change?
- What do we want to share with the rest of the company, with our partners, and with people further afield?

Care:

- Did we respect working conditions? After the intensity, who needs a rest?
- Did we pay everyone well?
- What didn't work so well? What do we do about that next time?
- How did we protect the environment through what we did? What could we do better next time?

# NOTES ON DIRECTING

Don't be afraid to step into the role, even though it can sometimes feel vulnerable being 'the director' in a collective piece of work. Directors are theatre-makers – we have a vision, we instigate and drive the process. We work collectively in the rehearsal room but we also know how helpful it is to have someone leading the room, keeping things on track and that bigger picture – why we are making the piece – in mind. Someone to facilitate everyone having a say and manage group dynamics. To be conscious of the whole creative team and keep everyone in the loop.

## Notes for rehearsal

- People's lives are complex and you have to allow for flexibility in the rehearsal schedule. Work to be accommodating.
- Ask people to come into the process, to experience, listen in and build with you. Try not to isolate yourself. Building with people can enrich the work. Trust the minds in the room – empower everyone to contribute and play.
- Focus on specific explorations on specific days and plan who needs to be there.
- Think about the process, the journey and how the show is being brought to life. Feed more in each day – themes, concepts, atmospheres.
- Create space – if a piece is getting too text heavy, create space for the audience to think and feel, allow time for something to happen. Directors can have lots of ideas and want to pack a lot in – but audiences need space to process and reflect.
- Boredom and emptiness can be interesting to watch, as can the mundane and the everyday.

- Try not to get stuck talking – put things on their feet. It's when you don't know what might happen next that exciting things emerge.
- Don't get too precious. Hold on tightly, let go lightly!
- Break the rules as soon as they become comfortable or familiar.
- Find the world you're in. Play with what that world offers. Then find the world within. Explore what's really happening within the world.
- If you get stuck, go back to what interests you about the themes and the context of the show you want to make. What are your desires and dreams for the piece? Why are you making it?
- Don't be afraid of the 'obvious' or supposedly cliched. Sometimes something is powerful because it's archetypal.
- Ask the opinions of people you know and trust, invite them in and ask for feedback.
- Share with a stranger and see what they make of it.

## Notes to self

- What are the thoughts in your head that undermine or sabotage you? Write them down and then write the opposite – change the lens!
- Write from the prompt – 'my duty as a director is to ...'. What do you believe in? What is your personal manifesto?
- Put your craft at the centre of your practice. Don't rely on your experience alone – keep learning, keep curious.
- Dream whenever you can. In between two jobs, while you're feeding the baby, at the pub, when you're with friends. Keep the dreams alive. Scribble in books, draw pictures, write stories, take photos, share voice notes.
- If something isn't working or you come up against it, sleep on it. Get perspective – trust that it'll work out. Try again tomorrow or the day after that.
- If you're co-directing, it has to be with someone you trust, and you have to be travelling in the same direction. Two voices are powerful. If you argue, do it behind closed doors – work it out away from the team and come back united.

# WRITING POLITICAL THEATRE (1)

## Aisha Zia

Aisha is a writer and curator, and the creative director of 62 Gladstone Street. Evie and Aisha became mates through a mutual good friend and worked together on An Indecent Incident, a play written by Aisha. The piece was an adaptation of a Dostoyevsky short story and was staged in an old zip warehouse in East London. They paid the caretaker with beer to let them use the closed top floor.

What I do when I first get a piece of testimony is read through it. A blind read with no attachments. On the second read, I highlight interesting words and phrases, and start to build feelings around the way this character thinks, feels. How they see/describe the world. I have to feel connected to them. I'll then listen to the testimony – not all of it, just sections of it – to listen to how they speak. I have an ear for phraseology and the words and intonations people use. I like to include them when I'm writing.

The important thing is to move away from the idea that this is strictly verbatim. That you must respond word for word. You have creative licence to write freely. Give yourselves permission. That can mean anything and, much like when writing poetry, you have to let it take you wherever it wants to go. It's an abstraction – shapes and colours, sounds. It should feel surreal and even absurd, at times. That's what theatre is. It's metaphysical reality. So, you have freedom to move with it, in and out of time and space. Let go.

The other thing that is important to remember is, text should always feel present. Like it's happening to us now – not in the past, but right now. It's urgent. It's not a retelling or a reliving (necessarily). It's the here and now. And that's how it effects people. You want your writing to get into people's bones, to creep up on them. To make them go places they've never been before, and to be held. To feel safe and brave, to feel scared and surprised. Ultimately, you want to move people and that's the trick.

My favourite anecdote from the time of *Our Glass House* is Evie calling me when I was fresh out of university (she was still on maternity leave with her son, who was barely three months old) and asking me if I wanted to do a play about domestic violence. My gut reaction was no. It was no because I thought 'I don't know anything about domestic violence'.

I don't say no out loud. I say yes. And this is one of those moments when I'm glad I followed another instinct completely. The writer's instinct. One that comes with curiosity and an openness to find out more. What happened next was that Evie sent me testimonies of female survivors she and Rhiannon had been interviewing in Bradford, Bristol and Cardiff. She also told me about her neighbour who had been in a horrific relationship and where an ambulance was called and the truth came spilling out. This is very much the feeling of *Our Glass House*.

And this is where we began writing. With real life. That's the creative impulse, to make theatre about real stories, and real people. I'd never worked like this before. I thought theatre was all about me. Or so I was told – writing plays was about an internal world, something that should come from the writer. That was wrong. The deepest connection I've felt as a writer is when other people's real experience connects with my own. And I want to tell that story.

What I hadn't realised before I started working on *Our Glass House*, was that I had been in abusive relationships – I just didn't know it. This was a shock to my system. And what I learned about working on this play and other plays afterwards is that theatre has the power to change people. But it only has that power if it changes you too.

The first monologue I ever wrote was responding to a deep connection with a testimony. I wrote 'Nicola' for *Our Glass House* and it transformed my working practice. I'd never written so vividly; my writing had never felt so alive and visceral. And that's because the interview was so honest, so clear and so raw. The art is in the process. What questions do you want to ask and why? This is how you're going to build your play.

We started with open questions and a premise. Why do people stay in abusive relationships and how do they find the courage to leave? What do we want to see? What do we want to say? How do we want the audience to feel? This is an interrogation. A controlled experiment. A devising process that is inclusive of text. It felt forensic and exciting, and some of my best writing is in this play.

*No Guts, No Heart, No Glory*, like all good plays, came from a conversation. The conversation was born off the back of *Our Glass House*, and the rapid rise of domestic abuse among young girls. We asked ourselves, who are the most marginalised teenage girls in the country? The answer was clear: Muslim women. I'd always wanted to do a play about teenage Pakistani girls, having been one myself. I'd also wanted to do a play in boxing gyms. My dad was a boxer when he was younger and my uncles were wrestlers in Pakistan.

I was having a conversation with Evie, and she said, 'Okay, let's do a play about Muslim women from Bradford who box'. Evie's mum's friend Alaa was a boxer. She also has 11 children. This shattered my stereotype of Muslim women immediately. And that's what we want. Challenge ourselves first. As luck would have it, Ambreen Sadiq, 16-year-old national boxing champion, and Saira Tabasum, universities champion, were also both in Bradford.

So, we began working. Unlike *Our Glass House*, where I was brought in during the devising process, this time I was part of creating the show from the start. Evie and I came up with interview questions, did many of the interviews together, cast untrained Pakistani Muslim female actors from Bradford and ran workshops with schools. After the R&D I moved to Bradford for six months to write the play.

The process of writing *No Guts, No Heart, No Glory* was different; it felt like my story. I was that young girl, fighting to be seen and heard. I was that girl who was told 'no, you can't do that'. It was hard growing up and I wanted to channel that energy into telling the story that eventually led to empowerment, knowledge and acceptance. *No Guts, No Heart, No Glory* is a play about empowering young Muslim women, subverting the media narrative. But it's also a play about being the best version of yourself.

# WRITING POLITICAL THEATRE (2)

## Rachel Trezise

*Rachel Trezise is an award-winning writer from South Wales. We were introduced to each other by John McGrath, then the artistic director of National Theatre Wales, and we collaborated on We're Still Here. Since then, she has written more theatre and fiction, and continues to work on new projects for both.*

Politics manifests in lived realities. Politics are always unavoidably present because people's local areas, countries, homes, incomes, socioeconomic status and everyday lives are profoundly shaped by the political system of the day. If you want to write political theatre that engages with your audience rather than threatening or lecturing them, it helps to introduce vivid characters and recognisable settings that your audience can relate to on a human level. We are comforted and empowered by seeing ourselves and our worlds represented on the stage. *We're Still Here* was told by working class characters and set inside a steelworks and a trade union meeting, sectors of society and localities often overlooked by traditional theatre. Demonstrating how gravely politics disrupts and alters the lives of vibrant, credible, empathetic characters will always reach and rouse more audience members than a theoretical speech or polemic. Music, comedy and popular culture helps too. Aim to entertain over and above educating.

Don't make a play a vehicle for your personal opinions. Political theatre should be about working with people who are affected by the political issues in question, not zip-wiring yourself in as a writer with your own preconceptions and ready-made plot. You want the writing to be truthful and to resonate with an audience who have experience of the topics you're dealing with. Talk to as many people as possible about the subject you're going to write about, noting the nuances and distinctions in their circumstances and concerns. Presenting a wide range of perspectives is more convincing than shoehorning your own view into your character's mouth (and definitely makes for more authentic dialogue). As the daughter of a former steelworker, I had plenty to say about the steel industry, but the *We're Still Here* community cast based in Port Talbot had much more recent and direct experience with the work and culture surrounding it. About 90% of the script was inspired by or came as direct quotes from interviews conducted with Port Talbot residents and/or community cast members.

I try to work towards giving the audience the material and tools they need to think for themselves in place of instructing them *what* to think. I would like people to leave the theatre with more questions than answers, and to be considering what they might do should they ever be faced with the same predicament as the characters they've just met.

When you're sure you've done enough research and you're ready to start writing, pitch your argument at your political adversaries. Doing this always helps me steer clear of demonising my enemies or over-idealising my allies. Even my worst political opponent is a human being with motives I seek to understand. Demonstrating respect for all sides should ensure no member of the audience is patronised, insulted or belittled by in-jokes or sarcasm. Writing inclusively rather than exclusively can open the door to new audiences. At the very least it staves off the tendency to preach to the choir. Test the strength of your own logic by playing devil's advocate with it.

Our current political situation did not come about in a vacuum. Today's politics are heavily influenced by the political strategies of the past, and what we do now to change or deal with our current affairs and crises will certainly influence the politics of the future. Try to make your argument more universal by setting contemporary specifics in a broader context – a brief historical overview can help the audience understand how and when this political fight began. In *We're Still Here* we referenced the long history of the steelworks in the area by including the workers' superstitions about an 800-year-old wall that stands on the grounds of the Port Talbot works. We also cited the decline of heavy industry on a global scale by including a short testimonial to steel plants that had recently closed across three other continents.

Finally, make sure you remind each member of the audience of their own political agency by exemplifying how capable ordinary people have been and continue to be at bringing about protest and change.

# HOW TO DESIGN AND BUILD A DIY SET

## Michelle Wren

*Michelle Wren is a socially engaged multidisciplinary artist whose practice is underscored by social activism. Evie and Michelle were friends from Goldsmiths University and squatted a London pub together after graduation, running it as an art exhibition/party/after-hours gig space. They have an attack-a-pella girl group, The Rusty Pins, together. Michelle has worked on multiple Common/Wealth projects as an artist and designer.*

**It's so much bigger than building a set.** When working on a conventional set-building job, you read the script and get told what is required by the director. But with a Common/Wealth show, you're listening to interviews with people and creating spaces for audiences to witness those stories. Sometimes, you're there from the start, participating in R&D, designing spaces in collaboration with the people making the show.

**Think on your feet.** When you're in it from start to finish, working collaboratively with people, you don't have to know what you are going to do in advance. You might be asked 'Can you do something with projection?' and you say 'Okay, I'll bring a projector and a camera and a computer and we'll see what happens'. You're constantly shapeshifting.

**Their rubbish is your gold.** I don't really like to buy materials. I get as much as I can from skips, builders' yards and scrapstores. I have one business I get pallets from, one business I get chipboard from, one business I get corriboard from. I get all my cardboard for free from a cardboard manufacturer. I literally drive my car into the back of the warehouse. The men in the warehouse know me and they load my car up.

For *Off Road*, the show Common/Wealth made about quad bikes, I rang round scrapyards and found one that let me gather plastic casing from old bikes. This was scrap which the yard would have had to pay to get rid of. We were doing them a favour. The back of my car was full of bike parts and this beautiful, colourful plastic casing from bikes. The young people knew what all the parts were because they fixed their own bikes up. Some scrap had old lights in, which I wired up to a battery. I made two seating areas using abandoned pallets. Apart from a few screws, a battery and bits of wood for frames, it was completely free.

I'm not opposed to buying materials but I think a lot of it is out there. Abandoned houses, scrapyards, recycling units, scrapstores, all full of so-called waste created by capitalism. We literally live in filth. There's a lot of stuff lying around. We draw artistic inspiration from the world we live in and we're making use of all the waste to create an amplified and artistic version of that world. We're not just replicating what we see.

Don't feel like you can't do stuff if you've not got money, because you absolutely can. There's so much rubbish out there to work creatively with.

At the cardboard place I use, the cardboard they give me is massive flat sheets, but it's offcuts to them. That is their waste. You just need to find out where the waste is.

What is someone else's rubbish is your gold.

**Never go to the office. Always go to the workers.** Make friends with your local manufacturers. Just actually go there and chat shit. Make friends with the people working there. I never go to the boss if I can avoid it. I'm a worker, so I feel more comfortable on the shop floor. In one wood shop there's this lad who works in the back who lets me take the scraps and they are really good scraps. If I'd gone through the office, they'd want to charge me for it.

Where I used to live, in Liverpool near the docks, there were warehouses everywhere. Doors were open and I'd be like 'What are you up to?' Everyone's bored in work so everyone wants to chat. People like chatting. You find out who's got what and you develop little dealerships. I'd be like 'I need one of these'. And they'd be like 'Go over there and speak to him'.

**Use cardboard.** It's free, and it's really easy to manipulate and work with. The set for the first show I made with Evie and Rhiannon was built from cardboard from the local IKEA skip. We made a big flour mill with a moving mill wheel out of big sheets of cardboard. There was this massive container overhead, all through the show, looming. We made these pulleys, and at a certain point in the show all this rice, representing flour, flew out of the container and the cardboard wheel span round. It was amazing.

**Use a rolling pin for a hammer.** I had never built a set before. We couldn't build stuff out of wood and we didn't have tools (I have tools now and use them all the time, but I had no idea then). We didn't have a hammer, so we used a rolling pin. We didn't have a drill. We didn't have any money. Making the set for that show completely changed my life.

**Buy your own tools.** When you start getting paid for work, buy tools. It might be a glue gun, it might be a drill. Put some of your money into getting your own kit. At the beginning, you don't have anything and you have to use everyone else's. And that's fine. But now, people use my tools. I invest in my own work and I like having my own kit. I just did a job and I loved the cameras I was using, so I spent 10% of my wages on buying some for myself. That's my kit now and I can use it to earn money.

**Get out of the studio – make your own space.** Make space for yourself, and remember, if you're making space for yourself, you're making space for other people. Finding, making and having space is so important. You need somewhere to work. It might just be the spare room. It might be the living room. It can be anywhere, but just know that it is important to have a space.

**Squat the lot.** When Common/Wealth asked me to build that first set, we were all squatting in Bristol. We were so free at that time and we were able to make art because we didn't pay rent. We were working class kids who couldn't afford to stay in these cities and squatting made it possible. We were making theatre and art and we were really proactive. Some of the people involved in those early shows had squatted a pub in London with me and Evie a few years earlier. We used to put on nights and do art exhibitions. We gathered the different artists we knew and got them to come and make work in the pub. Being young, not paying rent, being autonomous and not answering to anyone. Not needing funding, not needing to ask anyone for money. Not needing to be approved of or liked. Just being able to flow and be weird. It was mad and beautiful, and so many people from that era in the pub have gone on to do amazing things.

I learned how to think big with space from living in squats. If you work in art studios, you don't learn to think that big. In squats you adapt to the space you're in and you can build all sorts of stuff. We had these big buildings we were living and working in. It made you less afraid to take on a space.

I started to learn DIY in the squatted pub in London because we had to fix the place up – we were plumbing our own toilets and building things. I will believe to the bitter end in DIY art, DIY culture, squatting culture. It's about taking space – not taking what's not yours, but making use of empty space. Creating space for yourself and creating space for other people. You have to take and make space. You don't just get given it.

Even though the law has changed since then, you can still squat here in the UK. It is legal to squat commercial premises. And if you want to squat, the Advisory Service for Squatters (https://network23.org/ass/) will help you. The *Squatter's Handbook* on their website is the perfect place to start. It's affordable and tells you exactly what you need to know to go and get a building.

**Teach yourself and learn off others.** I worked for a circus company and we did massive set builds. There were a lot of carpenters there who taught me about tools. I would stand there and say 'I want to use this jigsaw but I'm scared'. They'd say 'I'll stand with you'. I got more confident and started to buy my own tools. I've got into working with video now. I taught myself video editing and projection as a way of putting my sets into digital worlds. I pretty much taught myself everything, to be honest.

**Don't be afraid of your own aesthetic.** It's so easy to think 'they can build stuff better than me', 'they can video-edit better than me'. But I've got my way. That's my niche, my style. If people don't want that for a job, that's fine – they don't have to get me on the job. If you believe in your own style, you'll find people who will want to work with that.

**Say yes.** Just say yes. Don't be afraid. Don't think that you can't do stuff. Say yes to stuff.

**Don't be afraid to ask.** Don't be afraid to put yourself out there. In the arts, there are a lot of people who put themselves out there and it's generally a certain kind of person. It's hard to access the arts if you come from a working class background, but maybe the tide has turned a little bit and more arts organisations want to work with people with your life experience.

**Don't be afraid of the fear.** Every job I take, I've got impostor syndrome. But everyone's got impostor syndrome. No one thinks they can do it. Some people handle that better than others. Believe in yourself. Say yes to stuff.

# HOW TO LIGHT PEOPLE LIKE ROCK STARS

## Andy Purves

Andy is a freelance lighting designer and was recommended to us by Lisa Maguire from National Theatre Wales. He came on board for We're Still Here, and we've worked with him ever since. We like his politics and how much he cares about every detail.

**It's a collaboration.** The ideas have to be there in the first place. Lighting doesn't have any meaning on its own. It's about people. The stakes for the people involved in the show must be high – only then can you interpret the feel of it, the tone of the story, the message. You need to have an eye on the poetry of the piece.

**You don't need lots of kit to light a show.** You can do amazing, powerful things, bold things, strong things, with very little resources. You can do a lot with a single £19 rechargeable floodlight from your local DIY shop. Whether you have a single light or a fancy lighting rig, the design principles are really similar.

One light can be very powerful. You have to make a really strong decision about when to turn that light on and what to do with it. It might be best to do the whole show with whatever light is available in the space, and then at the perfect moment, turn those lights off – darkness is one of your tools. Bringing that one light in to heighten a particular crucial moment. It might only be on for 30 seconds and that really could be the best use of your resources. It might be that you need a huge shadow, or that you want someone to look strong and direct. Where you put that light in relation to your performer – in front, above, below, to the side – creates very different effects.

**A one-light-only practical exercise.** Take some time to play with one light. It's all about how the light lands on the face and the body and the surrounding space. That's what gives you meaning. Trust your instincts and keep talking to each other. You can do this in any dark space with a small group of collaborators. It's better if you don't use a wired stage light to do this exercise. A phone torch or battery floodlight is perfect to move around safely.

1. One of the group stands in the middle of the room. Someone else holds the one light and moves to a position about a metre away from the person in the middle of the room, leaving the light turned off for now. Someone else finds the room's light switch. Everyone else – you're the crowd, there to watch and describe.
2. Room lights off. Big moment. Explore the darkness. It's the new base to your work. What can't be seen?
3. Switch on your one light and stay still – the crowd describes what they see, what it reminds them of, what they feel.
4. After a while, play with placing the light in different places around the body of the person – low down, behind, close, far away, to the side, above – each time keeping still. What's changed? Keep the descriptions coming – how is the scene talking to you?
5. Explore slowly shifting from neutral states to something more heightened or weird.
6. Grab a nicely atmospheric music track on someone's phone, ideally without a vocal. Use the structure of the music to inform some simple, slow movement with the performer and the light – as simple as someone walking in and sitting down for a bit then walking away. What can careful use of your one light add?

Trust that what you're sensing about what light is doing will be felt by others. You're creating a vibe, an atmosphere, and other people will feel that too.

**Let the space talk to you.** That's a big part of the thrill of creating theatre outside of theatre buildings. The ideas are built with the space. A huge warehouse or the corner of a classroom, the space writes the show, so you have to listen to it – not in a pretentious way but in a very practical one.

With *We're Still Here*, the production needed to be big, because the steelworks that form the background to the town are big. In the gigantic space, the interplay of light and staging pulled the audience around the space, directing attention and making the audience journey clearer.

It was a heavy and dangerous and muscular space, with rust, metal and concrete. We were working with this idea that there were ghosts in the rust and decay of the structures. We needed a bold, industrial feel to the lighting, but also something that could become otherworldly. Though we stayed away from on-the-nose ghostly kind of lighting, the young people lived in a shadowy world whereas the steelworkers lived in bright, working light, very clear, orangey or bright white. We wanted to create an idea of the kids being of the rust – they'd played and grown up around all this mess and decay. They were agile and comfortable around those half-lit structures, whereas everyone else was more nervy, exposed.

**Aim to heighten and hero.** *Peaceophobia* was about dreams and aspirations of people through car culture. We aimed at really heightening and heroing the cars. That needed a bit of fancy light. The show happened in multistorey car parks, spaces with no infrastructure for theatre, so the work was logistically complicated. That's where you need more resources and a team of people with clear roles. The ideas were bold, technical and strong, like the cars, and the lighting needed to go there too. The cars themselves 'talked' during the show – a challenge that was solved by lights inside the cars activated on cue, all done wirelessly. At the end of the shows in Bradford, the cast and audience were huddled together with these beautiful cars gleaming in the light and the sun setting on the horizon.

The show moved between normality and really heightened situations, from the three blokes talking about their everyday experiences to three amazing heroes, showing off their head-turning cars. We played with neutral light and colours, with intensity and saturation. A brightness that grabs the eye.
That echoed the vividness in those men's lives, with the show moving between the invisibility of a normal guy from Bradford to the massive visibility of a young Muslim man in a swanky, souped-up car with megawatt sound system, in terms of how they're viewed by the police. Invisible and hyper-visible at the same time – showing their exposure and vulnerability to racism.

**Light to contrast the ordinary and extraordinary.** *I Have Met the Enemy* was about the international trade in weapons and played in youth clubs. The space had to move between feeling like a normal hall to being extraordinary – from youth club to rave, jet bomber to Parliament, from living room to arms trade fair.

Sometimes we were just listening to the stories of the participants, moments that needed clarity, truth and simplicity. Systems of the military-industrial complex, of death, versus very simple human experience, of life. The show was about those tensions. We used lasers and all kinds of technology, but when the show moved into those lovely moments where it was just a person talking surrounded by ordinary people listening, there was a gentle, softer light on the performers so it didn't feel like they were different from the audience. It's all about shifting power and exposure. We cast a very soft, even light from all sides, making sure everyone was gently in connection with the speaker and the speaker only slightly brighter than the crowd. The aim is that nobody feels uncomfortable watching it. Nobody has a great big spotlight dazzling them. The comfort of the crowd is something that's always on my mind.

Sometimes, you're making a space for people just to be together. To talk, to share. You're not highlighting anyone; everyone's cast in the same light. Sometimes I bounce light off the ceiling, casting a diffuse general light and it feels like a room. And then suddenly, something happens that's strong and special. Light can really help move us between those states.

**Use light to enhance power.** When you're working with people that are new to performance, their voices become stronger and clearer as the show is made. Suddenly, someone stands on a chair and they're very different – they've got a different status and they're going to tell us something and they've got the power to do that. When we made Radical Acts, there were loads of conversations about not wanting to expose people too much, but once the performers felt confident they wanted MORE, not less, of that spotlight feel!

**It's like a band going on stage.** You may never get to a point where the lighting is fixed. Nailed down is not what Common/Wealth do. Everything's quite fluid. A traditional theatre approach tends to try to get everything locked in. With Common/Wealth, it's more like a band going on stage. It could be different every night. It should be different every night.

With Radical Acts, we made changes each day, in line with what everyone wanted. It's part of the politics of how the shows are made and it's what makes the shows feel necessary and important. Think about the process as more like a music gig, where you're responding to things rather than fixing them. Obviously, you need structure, but you're also improvising. There's a wildness to the process, but there's also the discipline of getting a message across. There are phases of wildness and freedom, interspersed with structure and clarity.

**Ask annoying questions.** Ask, what does it mean? What is this bit about? What do you want it to say? What do you want it to do? What are you trying to get across? How can I help with that? How can light, sound and everything else come together?

There might be an idea that has hung around for weeks and been rehearsed like crazy but it might not convey anything to someone outside the process. It may need a bit of help to jump out. To live.

# COMPOSING AND SOUND DESIGN

## Wojciech Rusin

*Wojciech is a composer and sound designer. We saw Wojciech performing in a pub in Bristol as Katapulto, with an experimental set involving props, televisions and sound pedals. We went up to him after his gig to ask if he'd make music for one of our early shows.*

When I make sounds for site-specific theatre, I respond to the script, emotions in the play and to the architecture of the site.

We started to use **'sound worlds'** to describe music and sound design in Common/Wealth shows, and it stuck. I think about the timbre or tone that is needed – is it aggressive? Is it soft? Are abstract sounds and processed sounds needed here or something more literal, recognisable? Electronic or acoustic sounds?

When we did Our Glass House, it made sense to use domestic objects as sound sources. I used a cello bow on drinking glasses, creating a high-pitched sound which had a penetrating and unsettling effect. You go through **a series of experiments, playing different objects,** and suddenly you're bowing a glass and it sounds quite interesting and resonates with the theme. The show explored domestic violence and the house became oppressive via the sound world.

With Common/Wealth shows, the responsibility for creating sound worlds is often shared, and so my role can be more about involving people and bringing them on board rather than doing everything by myself. Sometimes you have to be ready to let go of control over the sound. You create a composition that might make complete sense to you, but not make any sense to the cast or director. And then you have to say 'Alright, let's try something else'. They trust you, but they also have their own objectives – they want to emphasise the meaning of the words, maybe, or they have their own musical tastes and want to incorporate them into the show.

It's difficult to distil the process into general points of advice because **you're always responding to a specific place, finding ways to translate what you see into what you hear.** It really depends on the play.

**I'm not too technical, to be honest.** If it's too technical, the fun is gone. You can do it yourself with relatively little technical equipment, as with *No Guts, No Heart, No Glory*. But, as with *We're Still Here*, when you have a sophisticated technical infrastructure and resources, you can do things on a bigger and more complex scale.

## *No Guts, No Heart, No Glory*

We started the R&D for *No Guts, No Heart, No Glory* in a boxing gym in Bradford. The gym members were using these big, round rubber exercise balls for training and I found them fascinating. They were almost a metre in diameter. If you hit them with a percussion mallet, the sound resonates inside. I wanted to make a musical instrument that would not look out of place in a gym, so I gathered a few of those balls and amplified them with contact microphones. That didn't work very well – they just sounded like big rubber balls! Then I realised it would be better to treat them as an electronic drum set where, every time you hit the ball, the computer interpreted this as a note and played a sound. That way, the balls could play any sound you wanted – a vibraphone, marimba, a percussive sound or sampled breaths of the cast.
I built a whole drum set from the balls, with different sounds coming out of them. The whole set, which was quite big, could be deflated and put into a suitcase for touring.

I have never particularly played drums and I wouldn't consider myself a drummer. But if you have these big, inflatable balls, and you're hitting them with big sticks, the image created resonates with a play featuring boxers showing how they train, and how they are empowered as boxing women.

The balls were also great for workshops in places we toured to. You bang the ball, it plays a note in a scale. Participants could just play the balls and make a tune from a pre-programmed musical scale. The balls invite playfulness, which works well for people in a workshop scenario who are not musicians, and who may feel intimidated by a traditional instrument. Because the balls look so playful and weird, there is a kind of invitation to play, to try stuff out and not feel like there's a right or wrong way. It's such a weird-looking set-up that there is no judgement and no fixed technique for using it, unlike traditional instruments.

Over time, I expanded the system. There was a solo scene where one of the women is punching a punchbag. I installed a few contact microphones onto the punchbag, and these were triggered every time she threw a punch, playing a sample of orchestral drum, an epic kind of monumental, over-the-top sound. There was also choreographed, collective movement in the boxing ring. The floor of the ring is itself a suspended membrane – something that vibrates like a big drum. So, I hid microphones underneath it. The gestures and jumping of the performers were translated into sound in a very immediate way, creating a dramatic effect that worked for the high-energy moments.

The technical set-up was not expensive or sophisticated. There was an Alesis Trigger iO module, which costs around £100, and contact microphones are really cheap and small and you can glue them to objects with gaffer tape. The module translates the electrical signal from the microphones into a signal (MIDI) that the computer understands. You tell the computer that if a hit is strong, it should trigger a sample of a large drum, or if it's weak, it should trigger a smaller sound, like the sound of a triangle. I used

Ableton as the main software and not QLab which I guess is the standard for theatre.

There was a composed soundtrack, developed during the R&D and devising process. I would respond to the script and consult with the creative team to find out more about scenes where music was required. Constantly exploring, how can I support this with sound? I would bring some music to the rehearsal space, we would test it, and if it seemed to work, I would extend it, create variations or develop different motifs. Sometimes the cast responded to the energy of a track and it took them somewhere new. In this phase, you're just gathering feedback from people and trying things out on an intuitive level, without overthinking it.

In conventional theatre, the technician runs the lights and sound from QLab. They usually just press Play. I was doing a little bit of that, but sometimes I would play a live soundtrack or do some live mixing on top of the pre-recorded track. Sometimes the actors would play the instruments, and in that case, I would be adjusting the levels.

## *We're Still Here*

We were in a 130-metre-long abandoned tin factory and I wanted to make the building speak. The team installed electromagnetic hammers on the beams of the factory in two or three places – we were basically shaking up the building with these powerful electric hammers. There were scenes which involved the presence of ghosts or scenes of frustration and anger. In these moments the steel structure started speaking, resonating in a series of disorienting echoes. The gear used was a module called MIDI-RLY08. It translated MIDI notes from Ableton into electric impulses, creating a kind of giant electro-acoustic drum machine.

We transformed this abandoned factory into a musical instrument. This element of the sound design reminded me of the beginnings of industrial music in the 1980s, where bands like Einstürzende Neubauten or Faust would have chainsaws, power tools and concrete mixers on stage. This was industrial music in a very literal, direct sense.

There was a satisfaction in finding ways of playing the building and bringing it back to life. But then we had to find the scenes where it would work best. There was a scene involving a moment of frustration and anger from one of the steelworkers, an angry internal monologue. Here, the hammers worked best.

There were a lot of speakers and subs installed in the space. We used a multichannel system which allowed me to create complex sound design, with particular sounds travelling from one place to another, or revolving around the space. This was all programmed in QLab. I created the musical score with only string sounds. I was following a cinematic style, trying to illustrate the epic scale of the factories and machines. Certain scenes required a kind of symphonic sound. There's something quite particular about symphonic orchestration. It's very powerful – you have every frequency occupied and this creates a very intense sound world.

Playing this kind of score into this big space with quite a lot of natural reverb felt appropriate. The sounds resonated in the space for a few seconds, bouncing between the walls, slowly decaying into silence. There was a satisfying conceptual tightness about the whole thing. The string arrangements with almost romantic overtones juxtaposed with this literal, industrial drum machine and the view of the Port Talbot steelworks on the horizon.

# A BRIEF GUIDE TO MAKING SITE-SPECIFIC THEATRE

## David Evans

David is a freelance production manager and consultant who is particularly committed to making theatre sustainably and responsibly. David was Head of Production at National Theatre Wales when we worked together on We're Still Here. He's supported us in numerous ways before and since that show as an adviser and friend.

Site-specific theatre is an effective way to make a show. You can tell the story of a location much more profoundly than you can in a theatre. Think of Jeremy Deller's *The Battle of Orgreave*, when 1,000 people re-enacted the violence of the 1984 miner's strike in the location where it occurred. Think of Ann Jellicoe's Community Plays, written by communities and performed by those communities in their community. The form is powerful.

Fabulous though the form is, putting on a show outside a theatre has its challenges. But these are surmountable if you manage them in advance.

### The audience

Can the audience get there? This is rarely a problem if you are in a city, but smaller towns, villages and rural communities are usually less well served by buses and trains. Check when the transport finishes and if it runs on weekends. If there are restrictions, can you change the times of the show to fit in with public transport timetables?

Preferable though it is for people to use public transport, some will inevitably come by car. Can you provide sufficient parking nearby, and is there disabled parking close to the entrance?

Does your site have a postcode? People will use this to get there, and it's difficult to get deliveries without a postcode. If it does not have one (fields and mountains rarely do), is it easy to appropriate a postcode from a nearby building? An additional location system to consider using is what3words – free, simple to use and essential if you're working in rural areas.

Is the site accessible? Can you get wheelchairs onto the site comfortably? If not, can changes be made to provide access?

How the production is staged can make it difficult for wheelchair users and others. It is worth considering creating elevated viewing platforms that are strategically positioned to give an optimum view of the action. For *We're Still Here*, we used two viewing platforms and escorted platform users between them at appropriate moments so they didn't miss any of the show.

Some people have hidden disabilities and will need a seat, so have a few discretely set aside that you can hand out if needed. This can make a lot of difference to some audience members.

## Welfare

Are there toilets on site? If not, you will need to provide them, including sufficient disabled toilets. It's worth noting that toilet hire is relatively cheap; however, cleaning them is not, so it might make sense to hire more. Don't forget that your company will need toilets, and it is worth considering whether they should share with the audience.

You will need to be able to supply drinking water and have somewhere to do first aid if required.

## Company

There are fundamental things that you will not necessarily find at a location that you would in a theatre, but you need them:

- Dressing rooms, a welfare room where your company can take a break and eat. If there are children in the company, there are very strict regulations that you must adhere to, which will include separate dressing rooms.
- It is also important to provide somewhere secure for personal items.
- The production team will need an office.
- Your wardrobe team will need somewhere to do the laundry.

## Cleaning and waste

Just as venues have cleaners, you will have to provide cleaning in the public areas and backstage. Your show may generate waste, as may your audience. It is important that you have a policy for responsible disposal of this waste. It may help to talk to the local council about this, but there is likely to be a charge.

## Venue

Choosing your venue is crucial. It may be the reason that you are doing the show or you may just need to find somewhere to mount your production. Whatever the case, there are things that need considering. For example, how large an audience can you get in? This will depend on several factors and should take into account how many people you have in the company. The venue might have a performance licence already, but if not, you will have to work this out. Guidance for this can be found in an Association of British Theatre Technicians publication, *Non-Conventional Theatre Spaces*, which is packed with good advice (https://www.abtt.org.uk/).

## Relationship with the venue

It is so much easier if you have full control of the site, as sharing makes life much more complicated. A shared space might be a building, or it might be outside, but in all likelihood, you will be a visitor and should respect the other users, who may not be too delighted that you are there. It is important to be as easy-going as possible. Outdoor sites popular with dog walkers will require a 'dog mess patrol' before work can start, and many sites will require security to prevent theft and vandalism.

Avoid making changes to the building, even if you think that you are improving it. It is really helpful if you have a clear contract with the owner where both sides agree what can and cannot be done and who is responsible for what.

## Technical

Does the site have sufficient power? If not, you may need a generator, which is expensive, bad for the environment and will require a qualified electrician (also expensive) to set up. You will need to consider the generator's exhaust fumes, the noise that it makes and logistics for safely refilling the diesel. It is much more sustainable to design the show to use the power that is available, and much cheaper.

## Equipment

Can you leave equipment in place? It is annoying and expensive having to derig after a show and rerig the next day. Do everything in your power to avoid this. If you have to, think about storage on site and budget for the extra time it will take.

## Rigging

If you are suspending anything from the roof, you may need an engineer's report to confirm that it is safe to do so. The venue may have such a report already, but if not, you will need to commission one. If you are creating any temporary structure for people to use, these might also need an engineer's report.

## Licence

As of July 2024, a Temporary Events Notice is not required in England and Wales if you have less than 499 people on site, including the company, and you are not serving alcohol or showing films. In other circumstances, you will need to apply for one from the local council, which will not be unreasonably refused.

It is worth keeping the authorities informed about your activities even if you do not require a licence. It helps the police as they will know why there is an unusual gathering, and this should also avoid having the police visit your site at an inopportune moment. Similarly, if you are using fire, tell the fire service in advance.

## Comms

It's important to keep your audience as informed as possible, as they will be experiencing something that they are not familiar with. Communicate with them by email, have information on your website. You cannot tell them too much. Crucial information will include how to get to the venue – will it involve walking? If the show is outside, will they require suitable clothing and sturdy footwear? Should they avoid bringing bags? What is your policy for bad weather? Have you considered a 'wet weather version' of the show? It is prohibitively expensive to get wet weather insurance, so most companies prefer to go ahead whatever the weather. Tell the audience what access provision you have and encourage them to share any specific needs they may have so that you can cater for them.

However much you plan, you cannot control everything. The weather is unpredictable. The council may decide to dig up your main access road. Train strikes, illness – these things are all out of your control. However, the more that you do have planned, the more capacity you will have to manage the unexpected and have fun making your production.

# HOW TO PRODUCE (IN A NEIGHBOURHOOD)

## Chantal Williams

*Chantal is Community Producer at Common/Wealth, based in Cardiff. She has lived and worked in East Cardiff for decades and has been with us from the early days of our work in the city. She led the incredible grassroots dance collective, The Underdogs, with her mum, Roberta, for many years.*

Build relationships. Care. Be authentic. Speak up.

It's about care. I live here. I want to see stuff happening here. I want to see skills developing, from employability skills to artistic skills. I want to see people have an opportunity to leave here. I want that social mobility.

There is so much that we can achieve through the work. We realise how big the opportunity is. But we need to balance that against what can happen over time, rather than trying to do everything for everyone all at once. It's about realising what can be achieved and doing our best to make sure it has a positive impact.

East Cardiff, where I live and work, is a funny old place. It's detached from the city. There's over the hill, and then beyond the hill. It's not far, but it is far. The bus connections are a bit shit and we can feel disjointed from the city. There was a time when there was a good energy and buzz around the place and we had great youth workers who really wanted to make change. Then nothing for about 20 years. Just nothing going on and nothing happening. That stale energy sits around a place. To be changing the narrative and to be sharing space with people to talk about important things is a beautiful thing. The money is not being taken to make art for art's sake. It's going into the place, into the audiences, into creating long-term social change via hyperlocal investments. Beautiful, beautiful, beautiful.

## How to build an audience

Be in it for the long term – you'll build an identity that people in the area will slowly start to recognise and trust. I wouldn't ask someone to come and be part of something if they didn't show any interest. I don't want to get people to go somewhere just for the sake of going. I don't invite people if they're not going to enjoy it. Building trust with people and building audiences is about making people feel like they can be vulnerable – that they can take risks and try something new – and be confident that these things are for them as well. People say 'That's not for me' and I reply 'I know, it's not for me either, but also it is, because ...'.

Invest in the conversations that happen before the show. The first round of conversation is about letting people know what's happening and seeing what kind of interest there is. Even if there is just one small pique of intrigue, I do a double conversation. I'll double back rather than have the full conversation there and then. I'll tell them it's happening and line them up to have a look on the website, then speak to them again. We did some research which showed that at least 95% of the audience had at least one or two touch points before they came.

Chat to the community groups and local organisations to keep little pathways open and on fire, so that when the work does happen, there's lots to draw on. Dedicate time to maintaining those relationships. Every Thursday, if I can, I go out and meet with people for a cuppa.

There are two things that a community can wrap their arms around – the younger generation and the older generation. When we're working with the older generation, word filters down to younger generations in the community. And vice versa.

When talking to artists, advocate for people in the area. Artists love their work and that's amazing. But the people here may not. Ask the artists – what's the experience for the audience? Why are you making it? You really care about this work – you love it. I need to go and find these audiences, so I want to know who you are from the start. Who is it relevant to? Why should they care?

## How to create a Sounding Board

Our Sounding Board is a group of people who are from and/or care about the neighbourhood. They provide a conduit between ourselves, the place we are part of and the artists that work and visit here (see 'Sounding Board' in 'Works').

We have a desire to plant many seeds and create many fires in the area. Some of that is about investing in, inspiring and upskilling people by bringing them close to the arts, providing opportunities to work with artists and to travel to see work. Supporting them to make decisions about and advocate for the work and create their own thing. It is also about making space for people to network with one another, to share ideas and problem-solve. Creating opportunities for them to sit with artists and ask questions about their work in relation to this place.

To create a Sounding Board:

- Recruit from far and wide, find people who love the arts and the place. Get all those perspectives around the table.
- Work together to discover the function of the Sounding Board. Each context will be different and will need specific focus, skills and energy.
- Plan in social time. Get to know everyone. Go out for food. Talk with no agenda. Taking time to socialise helps build relationships.
- Go and see shows and art. Have a 'go see' fund so your board members can experience as many forms and approaches as possible.

- Include all kinds of practical training (we offered some British Sign Language training, which developed into front-of-house training leading to paid roles with the company). Decide this together. It can be creative or practical; think outside the box and about what skills might be transferable.
- Allocate resources – including people as well as money. Someone in your group needs to be thinking about and maintaining contact with the Sounding Board.
- Plan ahead so that the Sounding Board isn't an add-on – it's central to decisions you're making about the work that's happening locally.
- If you can, pay people for their time and at least cover expenses.
- Be mindful that your Sounding Board have lives and jobs and have given time to do something they're passionate about.
- Be mindful that when passion runs out, it runs out, and you may need to have a cup of tea and a chat. You need people actively engaged in the work. You can still be friends, take the kids out on a Saturday – the relationship is still there, but the work can move on.
- Recruit via social media, share it with local groups, etc., but also print it out and pop it in the local shops. People still look there for opportunities. Chat to people – at the school gates, outside Tesco, in the pub, through a friend of a friend. Find the people who want this as much as you.

# How to Produce (Outside of Theatre Buildings)

## Camilla Brueton, May McQuade, Ezra Nash

Camilla, May and Ezra are creative producers at Common/Wealth. May brings experience of work in Bradford on the DIY arts scene, and Ezra moved back home to Bradford from London to work (alongside May) on the Bradford 2025 City of Culture bid. Camilla is a visual artist and writer, working with us in Cardiff, bringing a range of experience in producing creative projects across socially engaged arts, charity, heritage and the higher education sector.

### Expect variety

Working as a creative producer, every week is different. You can be meeting people, writing funding bids, facilitating workshops, doing some creative facilitation, creating contracts, answering emails, planning timelines, researching for and planning new projects, thinking through logistics for an R&D, participating in an R&D, booking travel, sourcing equipment and finding people and things, writing risk assessments, organising the store cupboard, setting up space for a youth session, checking in with the team and supporting relationships. There are weeks when you're out and about, and weeks that are more office bound, doing what's needed to get a project to where it needs to be.

### Producers provide a holding space

Your job is to ensure that everyone is moving in sync. It's practical but is also about taking care of feelings and relationships. Teams often grow quickly when you are in a production phase and, as a creative producer, you set the vibes and make everyone feel safe and confident. Regular team check-ins highlight if anyone's feeling off key and encourage shared responsibility. As the spreadsheet you made is being carried out in practice, things can get busy, but being open to feedback is key. People will need care in different ways.

## When producing theatre outside of theatre buildings, everything is from scratch

At Common/Wealth, we often work with people making theatre for the first time in spaces not designed for performance. This can be complex, intense and inspiring. It means that, creatively, we get a blank page and can work without preconceptions. It also means we have to get to know the details. There is no template, so we need to find out how to heat the space, where the bus stops are, where the audience can sit, what the acoustics are like, who's around the space at night, what perceived 'threshold' there might be dictating how different communities feel about the space. We start a new story with input from the cast, funders, neighbours and our own research.

We build from scratch every time. Rather than liaising with a front-of-house team, we're deciding where and how tickets will be checked, even what table is used and what people will wear. This welcome is the first contact with the audience and we know how important that is.

## Be open to a different kind of conversation

When working outside theatre buildings, expect conversations that you wouldn't have if the work was taking place inside a gallery or theatre. With neighbours, cleaners, landlords and groups that often know the space way better than you. Listen.

## Set up clear agreements

If you're making a show in someone else's space – a shop, street, museum or even a theatre – set up clear working agreements beforehand, relating to how and when you can access the space, what you can take into it, what the owners or venue will (and won't) provide and any additional costs.

## Nudging forward

Listen to what everyone wants and help work out what is needed to make it happen. It can feel like all the tabs are open at once and that you need to keep all the data flowing in multiple directions. It's about caring, cheerleading, shepherding and nudging things forward.

## There's more than one way to be a producer

You can talk for days about what a producer does. Everyone has their own idea and everyone does it in a different way. Sometimes it's about being embedded from start to finish. At other times it's about finding the right people (a production manager, for example) and taking a step back to let them do their thing.

## Hold your nerve

You will learn as you go because every project is different. If you want to make work differently and in unusual spaces, there is no set format. You can't expect yourself to know it all. You just have to know how to look for it. There's always the first time you book a skip or organise a road closure, or work out what fast fashion is, or the regulations for chaperoning. With every new project, you are starting again. Just hold your nerve. And then google it and do it.

We draw on so many transferable skills. It's a privileged thing to have had any kind of artist training in the UK, and it's great, but you don't necessarily need that to do our job. If you've managed a group of young people, looked after a building, organised a family or booked a holiday, you can produce.

## Learn how to say no

Sometimes a no is a no. There's a grand idea, but then there is the reality of budgets or needing to get people in and out of spaces safely. But sometimes a no isn't really a no. Sometimes it's about finding a solution: 'I don't think we can do that. But what's another way to get to it? How can we do that? What's the stripped back version?'

## Be open to having a conversation about your role

We work with a lot of young people, and a lot of the time they don't know what we do. They say things like 'You're always here, but I don't see what you do'. Here's our reply: 'You knew you had to be here at this time and your travel was arranged. The building was ready and safe. We had a plan. There were refreshments. We had to contract and work with the people who own this space and negotiate what would be best for us, what we are allowed to use, what they are going to offer. How did we even get this idea in the first place? Where did the money come from? Who decided to give the money to pay for all of this? That person's being paid, and so is that person. They live all the way up there. They've been contracted and brought in to do this.' They then say 'I get it', and sometimes, 'Actually, that sounds great, maybe I could do that as a job'.

## Work with companies you trust and believe in

Work for a company you can get invested in. We know that many people don't get to work in that way. It's a privilege, but try and work for an organisation that you trust and that you can get behind the ethos of. It's so much easier when you really believe in why you're doing something. We are on board with the 'why'. The work has a bigger goal. Once you find yourself in a place where you're aligned with the ethos, that's where you do your best work.

## Decide whether you are going to work with your heart

If you're not going to work with your heart, that's okay – take it easy. You can work your nine-to-five and switch off when you switch off. But we're all working with a bit of our heart. Common/Wealth gets that out of us. We've committed to that. And we get it back. We've chosen for our job to be our politics and our community. We're really bothered about the work.

## Sometimes, do less, better

Set some boundaries on your working hours. We know it is easier said than done. We are often exhausted after projects. If you work in the arts, you're going to be doing long days periodically. Clock your hours. We rest after shows, going quiet for a couple of weeks. Get good at well-being checks. Remember, you have a life outside of work. Where are the days off in the project plan?

It's about being mindful that you can work long hours some of the time, but you can't do it all of the time. When you're working on different projects at the same time, make sure that you're not setting yourself up for burnout. We're getting better at it. Sometimes, do less, better. It's the right thing to do.

# HOW TO WORK WITH YOUNG PEOPLE

## Mariyah Kayat and Saoirse Teale

Mariyah is Speakers Corner Producer at Common/Wealth and, at the time of writing, is training to be a counsellor. Mariyah was a member of Speakers Corner from the age of 15, turning up in her school uniform after school to participate in our campaigns, festivals and plotting. When an opportunity to work as an apprentice came up, we met with Mariyah's parents to explain the role and Mariyah began a two-year apprenticeship, becoming Speakers Corner Producer afterwards.

Saoirse is Youth and Community Producer at Common/Wealth in Bradford and a theatre director in her own right. Evie and Saoirse first met when Saoirse was about 11 years old. Saoirse's mum worked for Women's Aid and had been involved in Our Glass House. In her third year of university, Saoirse volunteered on I Have Met the Enemy, then began working as a duty manager for Common Space, dreaming up Youth Theatre Lab during a shift one Friday evening.

### Think – why do we need this group in this place?

Think – what is needed in your city, town or village? In Bradford there wasn't a safe space for young people to come together, share ideas and create art or campaigns. Youth Theatre Lab and Speakers Corner filled that gap.

As facilitators, we represent two quite different Bradford communities, but both very Bradford. That really helps. We know more about the experiences the young people are talking about because we've lived them too, and our family and friends have all lived them. They don't have to censor themselves.

## It's not step one, step two, step three

It's not step one, get a building, step two, find the people. Obviously, that is what you have to do. But it's bigger than that. There's no easy formula. How we work, works for Bradford and for young people in Bradford. But how we work has also changed over the years and it will continue to change. The way it changes comes from the years of work and all the stuff we've been doing. It's responsive to the needs, interests and ideas of the young people. That's what drives it forward. It's an organic process.

## Sometimes what is needed is slow work

If you're working with people who don't know a lot about theatre, you can't be that regimented, it doesn't work. They won't come back, or they'll stay but have a rubbish time.

Spend time group-building, playing games, getting to know each other. Having a laugh. And doing karaoke. When we started Youth Theatre Lab, we'd do 40 minutes creative work, and then a lot of karaoke and dancing and eating pizza. Some of the girls loved singing. Even though they were from really different areas of Bradford and from really different backgrounds, they all loved Taylor Swift! They would scream and shout Taylor Swift songs into a microphone and be completely free for an hour. The kind of freedom that you can't find in many places any more, especially if you're young and in Bradford.

## It isn't always easy to engage a group

We were commissioned by Bradford Youth Service to make *Off Road*, a show about quad bikes and perceived antisocial behaviour among young people on a particular estate in Bradford. There was a lot of distrust on the estate and it was difficult to find young people who wanted to take part, even though it was a paid opportunity. We worked really, really hard. We were doing street outreach in four different youth centres in that area. Every night of the week, for about three or four months. We kept trying. The way we found the four performers who made the show was different in each case. We used all of our contacts to access people who might be able to help, we worked over a long time and we kept going.

## You've got to be in it

Whether it's for a campaign or for a certain topic or for a new performance, whatever it is, you need people who are in it, who want to commit to it, in whatever way and for whatever reason. That's why it works. Because there's so much care given by the people involved. It's about being together with people who want to be together and who want to work. You have to want it, otherwise it doesn't happen. You have to want to say things. You have to want to make a change, whatever that might be.

## Care about each other

We really have a lot of care for the young people. We go above and beyond. We email their schools. We set up meetings. It comes from the genuine care and respect we have, across the board, for all our young people. That's what sustains our projects and that's what keeps people coming back. They are well looked after here. It's very much like 'We care about you – you are important'.

## Make a plan but don't be rigid

We make a plan for each session, because otherwise we could just sit and chat. Sometimes, the plan will come from the timeline. On this day, we're doing this campaign or this festival, or whatever. What do we need to do in between? We delegate jobs. Who wants to design a flyer? Who wants to do the socials? Who wants to look at the budget and figure out what we need to buy? Who do we want to invite?

We respond to what we see and hear about how they are on that day. Sometimes we have a week where we don't get a lot of work done. Someone's had a tough week and they just need that support or that break. Sometimes you have a week that is super productive and everything gets done.

We're not rigid. It's not school and we're not bound by school rules. It's more free and open. It's really fun and we have a laugh and enjoy being together.

We have the vibe that if you don't want to do something, you don't have to do it. If you need to take six weeks out because things are really hard at home or exams are really stressing you out, fine, we'll see you in a couple of months. We're here whenever you need us. It's family vibes.

## Just talk

In both strands of our youth work, we've seen young people really struggling with their mental health in a big way. In the Youth Theatre Lab, we've got a lot of queer young people in the group and people who have transitioned while being with us. We have young, white, working class queer people, and we have young Asian Muslim people in the group, and we've had to navigate different kinds of beliefs. People ask, how does that work?

We just talk. It really is that simple.

Some people look at this group and say, how did you get them here? And actually, we never tried. They just came. And they just stayed. We like them all. We have developed a close bond. We've got good relationships and they bring their friends, their cousins, their siblings.

## Think – what's in it for the kids?

Who's your audience? What are your aims and ambitions? Are they actually reflective of what the kids want to do? What's in it for the kids?

## Be youth led – it works!

We're youth led. We don't sit here and say 'This is the programme, and you kids have to do it'. They decide and they choose. Give young people a budget and let them manage the budget. Teach them how to create a budget!

## Help the ones who want to make a career out of it

Not all of them are going to want a career in the arts and cultural sector. But the ones that do need that next step up, especially when they are from working class backgrounds, as they're unlikely to know anyone already working in the arts. Help them become a bit more savvy about the reality of working in the arts. Never pressure anybody to go into it, because it's hard. Never force it on anybody. Help them explore ALL their options.

Arm them with as much information and skills and confidence as you possibly can. If they are going to try and make it, whatever that might look like, get them access to all kinds of experiences. They have to know how it works. They have to know how to create a budget and how to write a funding application. Get them to practice how to talk about their skills, and how to put themselves forward for opportunities. Advocate for them. Teach them how to advocate for each other.

We really want to help build the next generation of young, working class artists, and we want and need them to be well equipped.

# How to Get Funding

## Ali Dunican

Ali is executive director at Common/Wealth. When Ali applied for the job, our paths had already crossed as part of her previous work at Quarantine. The job interview took place in a noisy Birmingham cafe, and we instantly knew Ali was the passionate, thoughtful and skilled person we'd been trying to find for years.

### Know what you want to do with the money

Be really clear about how you will use the money you have. That will help you find the right funder. Know how much money you need – make a budget so you can be sure.

### Research your funder

Find out what the money your funder provides can be used for. Funders are really clear about what they will and won't fund. Some won't fund core costs (only project costs), some will only fund capital costs (e.g. equipment) and some won't fund travel or food/subsistence when working away from home/on tour. Some funding for the arts is linked to social outcomes – community cohesion, improving health and well-being, for example.

Check who the funding pot you are interested in is for. Some funders will fund individuals, others won't. Some will fund companies and charities, but not individuals.

Read funders' websites, look at their accounts, find out who they've funded before. Don't just look at how to apply – read the whole website. There are clues in there that can help you, including words and phrases you can draw on in your application.

## Where to find funding opportunities

This will depend on where you are. Find out who is supporting art in your area. How are other artists getting funding? Create your own mini-database of possible funders. Join mailing lists and follow socials. In your research, include:

- Arts councils
- Local authorities
- Venues/arts organisations who might offer small amounts of funding or commissioning opportunities
- Funding sites – check out the free-to-use Funding Finder from Get Grants (https://www.getgrants.org.uk/funding-finder/)

To support new work in the arts, there are grants and there are commissions. Grants tend to come from arts councils, local authorities and charities (or trusts and foundations). Arts councils are organisations tasked by governments to support artists and the arts in their region or country. The funding they have to distribute comes from the government, through taxes or lotteries, and is distributed in line with what is called an 'arms-length' principle. This means that the arts council is supposed to make decisions independently of government policy.

There are several ways that commissioning happens. A commissioner (festival, venue or arts organisation) might say 'We really like your work and we're interested in working with you – let's talk about what we could do together'. And then there are open calls issued by commissioners that you can apply to.

## Where to start?

If you've never had any funding before, start small. One of the first funds an artist might apply to is an arts council creative development fund, or something similar. These tend to be small pots of money that allow you to do an R&D, access some training, travel somewhere to research and observe another company, or work with a collaborator.

## Be prepared to speak about your work with anyone, anywhere, anytime

Always be aware of who you're talking to and be prepared to talk about your work. Even when queueing for a ticket or a sandwich! And always remember that the people you meet as assistants now may be programming festivals and venues in a few years' time.

For some artists this can be easy. But others may need to work at it. Not everyone is socially comfortable at a pre-show reception or networking event.

It's always about being yourself, whoever you are and wherever you are from. After many years working in the arts, I notice – when developing relationships with partners or funders – that it's the human stuff that matters.

You're reaching out to a funder or commissioner because you have something they need, and they have something that can help you deliver it. Establish what you have in common and build that trust. Once you have that, you can begin to go, okay, what can we do together?

When you have conversations with people, you realise they're not so scary. They are human. If you can get to that point, and they have funded or supported you once, hold on to them as long as the relationship works and your remits match.

## What you will need for a funding application

- A budget that gives details of confirmed and expected income and expenditure for your project/activity.
- A few paragraphs that describe you and your artistic practice, background and experience.
- A description of the project or activity you want to undertake.
- How your project meets the criteria of the funder.
- How you will know whether you have been successful (how you will evaluate your project).

## How to create a budget

Think about 'income' and 'expenditure'.

Your income includes other grants, your own resources, money that a partner is putting in and income 'in kind' (e.g. space offered for free by a local organisation).

Your expenditure might include your fee or salary, fees for your team, travel costs, venue hire, box office and front-of-house costs, access costs, production costs (which might include materials, hire of equipment, insurance). You might need to spend money on communication and marketing. To find out how much things cost, do some desk research. Research online or phone people up to get quotes.

To work out salaries and fees, find out what others pay and consult relevant rates of pay at formal organisations like unions (e.g. Equity in the UK). Talk to people, propose a daily or weekly rate and discuss. Funders want to see that you are paying fair and appropriate rates.

A lot of new artists tend not to pay themselves or pay themselves quite a low rate in their first grant application. Try to pay yourself the going rate for your career stage. If that is just not feasible, consider whether you can – and for how long you are prepared to – work without money or limited fees.

Are there any other ways of raising money that will allow you to do the work you want to do? Part-time work? Freelance work in another skill area, allowing you to cross-subsidise your artistic practice?

## How to create a first draft of an application

When first setting out to make an application, some people just blurt it out. Others will create bullet points and craft them into sentences. Others will carefully craft it in their head before committing to writing. For some, the idea is only formed when they actually write something about it. Sometimes I've talked the application through with a friend and asked them to write down the key things I've said and used that as a starting point. There's no right or wrong way.

Answer the questions in a way that meets the funder's needs. You might be asked to explain how your project meets a key priority for the funder, and you never actually have the opportunity to describe the project in any detail. From the funder's point of view, there needs to be evidence that the project meets their needs. They will tick off their criteria against your application, and you want them to feel excited about your idea.

You've poured your heart out and described your project beautifully, then realised you've written far too much and need to cut out half the words. Brief accounts and good editing are called for. Give yourself a few days between drafts so you can see all those words that you don't need. Take note of character and word limits in advance so you don't have so much to edit. Be aware that character counts usually include spaces, and that when you cut and paste information in, most online forms actually accept fewer characters.

## Ask other people to read your draft

Once you've written something, sleep on it. Return to it after a day or two and re-read it. New ways of describing things crop up if you create space. Do this a few times.

Place your draft 'side by side' with the funder's criteria. Tick off where you've provided what they've asked for. Make sure you've covered everything. Imagine your funder doing the same thing. You want them to go through your application ticking things off – yes, yes, yes. Tick, tick, tick. If you make it easy for them to say yes, they will love you. Go for the easiest route to yes.

Arrive at a polished draft and ask someone else to read it. Does it make sense? Does anything need clarifying? If possible, ask them to read the funding criteria as well.

Ask people from funded organisations to read your draft – people who are already being paid, especially from venues, who aim to support other artists.

Carry on editing and refining.

Submit well before the deadline if you can. Be aware that some funders bring forward their deadlines if a maximum number of applications have been received. This should always be stated in their guidelines.

## Submitted your application? It doesn't stop there

Once you've done one application, you'll have lots of good information in one place and the next one will be quicker. But never just cut and paste from one application to another. Each funder needs a bespoke approach.

If you're successful:

- Say thank you.

- If it's a requirement, credit your funder in your work (a handful of funders actively don't want to be credited).
- Be sensitive and respectful – if you've been successful as part of a national scheme, be aware that the day of announcing who did and didn't get funding can be difficult for others.
- But when the time is right, let people know about your success, on socials and on your website, etc.
- Make sure you deliver everything you said you would.
- Invite the funder to whatever you're making and give them a decent amount of notice (ideally, six to eight weeks).
- Keep in touch – let the funder know how the project is going from time to time. Funders want to do good things with money. You've come along with your idea and they've thought 'That's what we want this money to be used for'. You're in a new partnership now, so stay connected.
- Don't forget the formal reporting bit.

If you're not successful:

- Try to get feedback, and work out how you could have improved your application.
- Make a note of when you might apply again.
- Look at who did get funding and try to figure out what they did differently.
- Carry on making work and talking about it. If a funder has seen your work, if they've seen something written about you, or heard other people talking about you, they'll take another look.
- Keep going and try again. It can take multiple attempts to get funding from some funders, even if you're a good fit.

## A brief note on alternative modes of application

Sitting down and writing an application, and writing in English, doesn't suit everyone. If you're considering using a voicenote or video, prepare it in the same way as described here. Address the funding criteria. Make it easy for them to say yes.

## Do it proportionately

Getting money to make art is hard work. It takes a lot of – often unpaid – time. You have to put a decent bit of effort in but you've got to do it proportionately. At the end of the day, trying to raise resources for art is about relationships. Make clear decisions about where to place your energy and allow this to shift at different points in time. Put your energy into funders who have criteria that you can meet, rather than those you really need to stretch for.

## It's a creative process

When you're fundraising, you're shaping the work. You're telling the story of the work in a different way. Don't be funding-led, in the sense of adding in ideas to meet the funder's rather than the project's needs. But as you start to tell the story of the project for a funder, you often find a new thing that adds something to the original idea. That's not tying yourself into knots to fit criteria. It's about shaping and making sense of an idea. There's a really creative and collaborative element of fundraising. It's about dropping things in and seeing if they fly.

## Ali Dunican

The idea of 'touring' is appealing. Taking a show on tour means more people can experience the work, the investment in the work is maximised and there's 'value for money'. That said, at the time of writing, touring in the UK is extremely challenging, and some might say there's no longer a touring 'circuit' to work within. Work is expensive to present. Venues and festivals often can't afford to take it – the financial risk is too high and, even if they do take the work, it's sometimes difficult for them to give it the attention it might need. All these challenges intensify if the work is by new artists.

Touring is generally resourced through fees from partners – venues, festivals or other organisations that accept touring work. They – or artists touring the work – tend to generate income to cover touring costs from grants. Money is generated through box office income but touring is rarely supported through this alone. If you're offered a fee, the partner will usually keep the box office income.

More recently, the idea of 'concept touring' has emerged, addressing environmental, financial and social concerns. The aim is to maximise being in a place, do more while being there, stay longer, have a bigger positive impact and reduce negative environmental impact. Especially when touring outside the UK and Europe, where travel by air might be the only option.

Concept touring is probably less about 'touring' and more about 'restaging' the work in a handful of places, travelling with fewer people, collaborating more with local artists and production teams, sourcing locally rather than transporting set and equipment, upcycling sets and infrastructure, hiring rather than buying.

But this approach is not without its challenges – it demands collaboration with partners who have a similar approach, the right contexts, resources and, critically, people who want to make it happen. There's more legwork in advance for local partners, but it can end up creating a new community (of collaborators, performers, associates, audiences, volunteers) for a venue or host organisation and can therefore have an enduring impact. Touring and/or restaging work can have a positive artistic impact, providing opportunities for artists to refine and reshape work, responding to what worked and what didn't.

Developing partnerships for touring/restaging work can take time. Let partners who previously presented your work know about your latest project – might they want to be involved from the outset as a co-commissioner? Or as a presenter? Invite them to see sharings, works in progress, first nights. Share video documentation if they can't make it in person. Ask promoters you know if they think the work would fit elsewhere and ask for introductions.

Think about artists or companies that your work might be similar to. Where are they presenting their work? Find the best possible ways to introduce yourself to new partners – an email or in-person introduction from other promoters or artists, a networking event you know they'll be at. Many venues and promoters are trying to be more transparent about how they programme work and often have artist events or information on their websites about how to approach them.

The work you make is your very best opportunity to attract the interest of others, so make the most of when you are presenting work. Invite those who you'd like to see it, giving them loads of notice.

It can be challenging to open a show and at the same time turn your attention to guests. Try to invite potential partners to the second or third performances and have other trusted people around you who can look after guests, so you don't feel totally responsible for them. But do make sure you speak to them, and that you follow up with them later by phone or email.

When considering potential partners, ask yourself:

- Are they interested in what you're trying to do?
- Are you making something they want and need?
- Is it the right place/context to present your work?
- What's the rest of the programme like? Will your work fit or clash? What does it suggest about how they will think about your work?
- What are the organisation's values, behaviours, culture?
- Does it feel like you could work together (with the organisation, and with the individuals)?
- Could you work alongside their rhythms?
- Can you collectively make the money work?
- Can they support in other ways (with rehearsal space, tech support and personnel, marketing support, etc.)?

Also, ask other artists – what it's like to work with them?

If you both decide to work together, there's often a 'spinning plates' moment that can last for some time – holding conversations to see if it's a fit and if the money and practicalities work. Sometimes you'll be doing this with several partners, who all might be at different stages. It's important to record all this information so you know where you're up to with each partner.

# HOW TO WRITE A PRESS RELEASE

## Catrin Rogers

*Catrin Rogers is a bilingual communications specialist with masses of experience of working across the creative and cultural sector in Wales. We first met Catrin when she worked with National Theatre Wales and she led on press for We're Still Here. We have since worked with her on multiple projects.*

As a means of telling the world about your extraordinary project, press releases, even in the digital age, remain an integral tool in a project's marketing campaign. A concise, well-written release can make a far greater impact than an expensive poster campaign – but there's an art to writing them. Most editors (arts or otherwise, professional or not) receive hundreds of emails a day, so making yours stand out takes some objectivity and ruthlessness.

Overall, a press release should follow the format and style of a news story. The more it reads like it's already a (genuine) news story, the more likely a journalist is to pay attention and respond to it. And that, after all, is the goal.

In practice this means that:

**The most newsworthy element of your project must be in the headline – and echoed in the opening sentence of the release**

How can you tell what's most newsworthy? Consider that old phrase beloved by journalists: man *bites* dog. A story about a dog biting a man isn't news, but a man biting a dog? That's out of the ordinary. So, if it helps, think of the first few paragraphs of your press release as a triangle:

- Headline and first sentence – short and sweet, making one (newsworthy) point.
- Second sentence – giving more context, crediting and perhaps elaborating.
- Third sentence – more background and less newsworthy information, but important to include.

... and so on.

It can be hard, but think as objectively as you can. 'Theatre company makes theatre show' is not news, but 'Theatre company makes theatre show with real-life steelworkers' is likely to make people sit up and pay attention.

Here's an example:

---

## COMMON/WEALTH & DUCKIE BRING THE POSH CLUB TO ST MELLONS COMMUNITY CENTRE

Theatre-makers Common/Wealth are working with Duckie to bring their hugely successful Posh Club to a community centre in Wales for the very first time.

The Posh Club, which Duckie have hosted in locations across their native London and the South East of England for almost a decade, is a tongue-in-cheek 'posh' 1940s afternoon tea featuring raucous live cabaret performances by local artists, waiters in black tie, vintage crockery and plenty of dancing.

## Avoid marketing language

Remember that for journalists, even arts journalists, facts carry greater currency than opinions and adjectives. Any artist might describe their shows as *brilliant, hilarious, unmissable* – but that vocabulary is better suited to marketing copy (which is aimed at the public). Press release copy must say (rather than describe) what is distinct and remarkable about a project (e.g. that it has won awards, that tickets are free to local residents, that it was created with a particular community, that it was written in response to a news story).

## Keep it short and snappy

Large files clog inboxes, and the longer a press release is, the less certain you'll seem about what makes your project stands out.

As a rough guide, anything longer than two sides of A4 is probably too long. Keep any biographies short – or better still, say they're available on request and just mention one or two highlights (if, say, your cast includes an actor famous for one particular previous role). Your collaborators may jostle for space but hold firm – the play's the thing, not what your lighting designer did in college eight years ago.

Embed URLs to relevant websites. Got a long list of tour dates and venues to include? Put them in columns to save space. Don't use two words where one will do. Include the key messages you want to put across about your project (e.g. the political call to arms, the community engagement, the unusual location), but don't waffle.

## What else to include (if you have it)

- A brief quote or two (no more!) from key creatives (where they can be more descriptive, but avoid hyperbole).
- Co-producer, key creative and funder credits – it's right and proper that you include them in your release. Keep them

towards the bottom though, and always check the spelling and crediting agreement.
- Any accessibility information.
- Age guidance.
- Ticket prices (but no need for great detail – e.g. if a show is touring, no need to list the prices in every venue).
- Finally, a brief synopsis of the listing information (show title, producer credits, dates, website URL) so that, if nothing else, a journalist can copy and paste these.
- Always include the contact details of whoever is managing your press at the bottom.

## Final touches matter

Think of the community you're trying to reach, and the media through which you'll reach them – would it help to translate the release into one or more other languages? Or make a large print version? How about making slightly different versions – for example, one with technical jargon (for tech media) and another without? Or one for local press and another for national press, with perhaps more context?

A news story is nothing without images and/or videos. In order to send them to journalists, it's best to embed a link to a downloadable folder of images (don't be tempted to attach them).

Copy and paste your release into the body of an email AND attach a Word copy, so journalists can read and use the text as they please.

Now go forth and spread the news!

## Simon Casson, Duckie

Simon Casson is producer for Duckie (https://duckie.co.uk/) and the Posh Club (https://theposhclub.co.uk/). We first heard about Simon through our friend Sarah Fielding at the Invisible Circus, and subsequently collaborated with him and fellow Duckie producer Dicky Eton to bring the Posh Club to Cardiff.

Apart from the rare occasion when it's the dog's bollocks, I bloody hate the theatre. Sitting in the stalls, trapped in my seat, in the dark, like a factory farm chicken, being punished by art.

Being raised as a lower working class kid from a council estate in Hackney, I was not entirely au fait with the iambic pentameter, and more drawn towards the dancefloor than a fourth-walled, buttoned-up chamber piece written by some cunt from Trinity College Cambridge.

In cahoots with Common/Wealth, Duckie run a regular cabaret event for older people in their nineties, eighties, seventies and sixties called the Posh Club. It's specifically made to appeal to local working class folk in St Mellons in East Cardiff.

It's sometimes easier to define the 'working class' for this age group – the golden and boomer generations, born in the mid-20th century. With half of the population now going to 'university', class definitions have become a bit more culturally unsteady.

We are proud of the Posh Club audience, but are finding it harder to nail drawing a predominantly working class audience for younger generations. There are lots of reasons why it's harder to serve this demographic but that won't stop us trying.

Rhiannon asked me to write a manifesto to make theatre that can reach a working class audience. Not for people like me and Rhiannon, and probably you, dear reader – from a working class background but pretty arty, with half an education, not completely marginalised and armed with a bit of so-called critical thinking.

Is it £10 tickets for *Tristan and Isolde* that are needed, or a genuine connection with authentic, bespoke form and content?

This post-posh-mini-manifesto has 10 rules, so here goes.

## Rule number 1: Make it for the people

Make a live love letter to the van drivers, the shop assistants, the call centre workers, the plasterers, the plumbers. Make a performance mixtape for the hairdressers, the ravers, the football fans, the reality TV lovers, the care workers, the prison leavers, the nail bar technicians and thems that hang around outside all night chemists. Make and show something they might like. Ask them what they think of it and listen to what they say. Serve them, don't swerve them.

## Rule number 2: Never do theatre in the theatre

Do theatre where people live, and make it site-specific. Do it in the community centre, the pub, the park, the street, the swimming pool, on the back of a lorry, on the beach, in a tent, outside the betting shop, on the local skating rink, in someone's sitting room. Treat arts centres as the last resort.

## Rule number 3: Serve the punters

Use theatre to serve people's lives, not the other way around. Don't be a genius in your garret, and get your hands dirty with the craft and graft of service.

Like doctors, artists should be in service to their communities. Host people. It's not just what's on stage, it's everything. Don't do it on a wet Wednesday night when everyone is too knackered after work. Put it on at Christmas, on Saturday nights, on New Year's Eve, Valentine's Day, Halloween, summer bank holidays, during International Itchy Genitals Awareness Week, on a month of Sundays, on Bonfire Night.

### Rule number 4: Unity in the Community

Be social engineers and put on a show that unites folk and brings them together. The queers and the old dears. Black and Brown and white unite and fight. Bring the street together, like the church used to do. Church halls and community centres would welcome you if you encourage strangers to become friends.

### Rule number 5: Give 'em the old razzle dazzle

Theatre is magic. It's not just actors mechanically reciting learned lines on a wobbly set. Give it some wow factor, that's our job. Be bold, use spectacle and show the audiences things they have never seen before. More Mary Poppins, less Harold Pinter. Use the big three popular forms – music, comedy and dancing. Make the characters big. Get a bit lairy. Large it. Most working class folk have a big character, unlike middle class people who wear muted tones and talk quietly in restaurants. Brecht wanted his actors to tell stories like blokes in the pub, be mimics and put the characters in inverted commas.

### Rule number 6: Variety is the spice of life

If you are genuinely talented, like Rhiannon and Evie, you can put on a proper theatre show, with a narrative and everything. If in doubt or, like me, you lack talent, put on a revue and book a few turns. A little bit of this and a little bit of that. A tightrope walker followed by a soprano followed by a magician and an Elvis impersonator (everyone loves Elvis). Mix street dance with classical music and add a short bit of incomprehensible performance art just in case someone from the arts council comes to see it. Put a tribute act on next to a piece of cutting-edge contemporary dance.

## Rule number 7: Show flesh

Everyone likes nudity, not just perverts like me. And if they don't, shock them a little bit and give them something to talk about the next day. Theatre is a carnal pleasure. Press the flesh, show the flesh, sink the pink. Use the techniques of performance art. Be like Katy Baird and take your clothes off 'to make a point'. This is best and most equitable with a queer audience and can be harder with patriarchal punters raised to believe that other people's bodies are their property. If this is the case, put on loads of nude men, and see what happens.

## Rule number 8: Get coin

This is the hardest one: how to fund it. If the gig genuinely reaches those who never go to the theatre, you've got more chance of moolah from the councils, lotteries and trusts. Do run your own bar, have a silent auction, sell badges, have a fundraising disco or jumble sale – but without funders' support, it's hard to do something ambitious.

## Rule number 9: Feed the punters

Give your crowd afternoon tea or Sunday roast or fish cakes or things on sticks. Host them like they are at your home. Get them a bit drunk for a laugh.

## Rule number 10: Dream big

What would you really like to do? What sort of thing do you really want to go to? Stage the Olympic opening ceremony on a teaspoon? Put on an opera in your back garden? Do it on ice? Make a DIY musical with your sister's band?

Be a collective joy rider.

Rise like lions after slumber, in invanquishable number, and fire up the dancefloor to bumber.

9 *The Posh Club*, Cardiff, 2023. Credit: Jon Pountney

11 R&D for *I Have Met the Enemy*, Cardiff, 2019. Credit: Jon Pountney

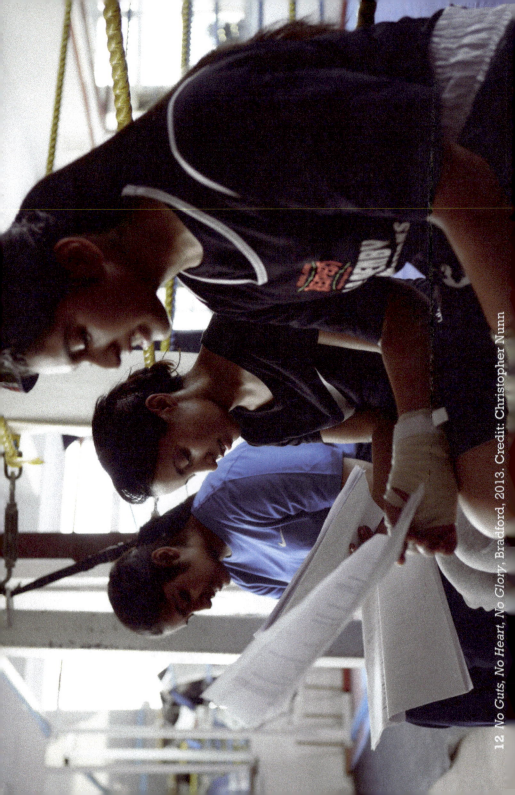

12 *No Guts, No Glory*, Bradford, 2013. Credit: Christopher Nunn

13 *Class: The elephant in the room*, Cardiff, 2017. Credit: Jon Pountney

***Read on for:*** *notes on works made over the course of Common/Wealth's life, starting with a timeline that maps our story onto the shifting political landscape.*

This section complements the reflections on our work in the book so far, adding details on seed, context, site and process. We've tried to avoid repetition and have not attempted to give comprehensive accounts – just enough to bring each work to life and share some of the learning. Look out for occasional contributions from performers and company members, providing deeper perspectives on the process. Please look on our website for more on each show and initiative, including videos, photos and description.

# TIMELINE

This timeline gives an overview of our work, highlighting the political shifts that we have responded to over time (it is not a comprehensive list, either of our work or political events).

|  | Political events | Common/Wealth activity |
|---|---|---|
| 2008 | Global financial crisis; Gaza massacre/Operation Cast Lead in Gaza | We are part of the DIY culture scene in Bristol and London, making with collectives of artists and activists; Common/Wealth is formed |
| 2009 | UK prime minister Gordon Brown leads global bailout of the banking and finance sector | *The Ups and Downs of the Town of Brown* (Bristol); Rhiannon tours with Circus 2 Palestine |
| 2010 | UK election sees a Tory–Liberal coalition take power; Austerity adopted as long-term economic policy, leading to cuts in public services and welfare | Rhiannon returns to Palestine visiting West Bank and Gaza; Evie gets pregnant |
| 2011 | Arab Spring; Occupy movement; civil war in Syria; UK riots triggered by Mark Duggan's death at the hands of the police | Common/Wealth formally registered as a company; Evie moves to Bristol with her six-month-old baby; work starts on *Our Glass House* |
| 2012 | Increasing pressure in our communities created by austerity | *Our Glass House* (Bristol); Evie moves back to Bradford |

| | | |
|---|---|---|
| 2013 | Introduction of a 'bedroom tax', penalising people on benefits for having a spare room in their house | *Our Glass House* tour; *No Guts, No Heart, No Glory* R&D |
| 2014 | Israel's military assault in Gaza leads to most lethal period of occupation for decades; mainstream media focus on British Muslim girls joining ISIS; Black Lives Matter (formed in 2013) grows even bigger following police murder of Michael Brown in the US; Saudi Arabia launches air strikes in Yemen using weapons made in the UK | *No Guts, No Heart, No Glory* (Bradford, Edinburgh, Manchester); Rhiannon moves back to Cardiff |
| 2015 | UK election sees a Tory majority win, led by David Cameron; long-time left-winger Jeremy Corbyn becomes Labour Party leader; Well-being of Future Generations (Wales) Act passed by Welsh government | *No Guts, No Heart, No Glory* UK tour; Nationalisation R&D in Bradford and People's Platform R&D in Merthyr Tydfil with National Theatre Wales (leading to *We're Still Here*); *The Deal Versus the People* (Bradford) |
| 2016 | UK votes to leave the European Union (Brexit) and Cameron resigns; Save Our Steel campaign in Port Talbot | *No Guts, No Heart, No Glory* international touring; Speakers Corner starts |

| | | |
|---|---|---|
| 2017 | UK general election triggered by Brexit fallout sees a narrow win for right-wing Tory party, led by Theresa May; Labour increase their Parliamentary seats with socialist manifesto; populist right-wing businessman Donald Trump becomes US president | *We're Still Here* (Port Talbot); *CLASS: The elephant in the room* (Cardiff); *Take Your Place* (Chicago); Common/Wealth receives Elevate funding from Arts Council England |
| 2018 | 'Punish a Muslim Day' – anonymous letters sent to people and businesses in Muslim communities | Common/Wealth joins Arts Council England National Portfolio; *Radical Acts* performance and interventions; Evie and Rhiannon receive funding from the Paul Hamlyn Breakthrough Fund |
| 2019 | Populist right-winger Boris Johnson becomes UK prime minister | *I Have Met the Enemy (and the enemy is us)* (Bradford, Newcastle); *From the Crowd* (Peterloo commemoration, Manchester) |
| 2020 | COVID-19 pandemic; international resurgence of Black Lives Matter movement following police murders of Breonna Taylor and George Floyd in the US | Bradford – Common/Wealth move to Common Space; *Peaceophobia* R&D and Sisterhood project with Speakers Corner Cardiff – Llanrumney base established in Cardiff; *Us Here Now*; collaboration begins with Moving Roots – a collective of arts organisations committed to developing new ways to make, tour and stage live performance; Sounding Board established in East Cardiff; Rhiannon gets pregnant |

| | | |
|---|---|---|
| 2021 | 'Culture wars' led by populist right political sects against the perceived dominance of liberal-left perspectives in arts, culture, education and media sectors | Bradford – *Peaceophobia* and *Sisterhood* premiere (also Manchester); *There is an alternative* exhibition at Common Space<br><br>Cardiff – *Payday Party* by Darren Pritchard, with Moving Roots |
| 2022 | Russia initiates a full-scale military invasion of Ukraine; cost of living crisis; UK government passes the Police, Crime, Sentencing and Courts Act, introducing sweeping police powers over peaceful protest | Bradford – Arts Council England portfolio funding renewed; *Peaceophobia* UK tour; *You are here as a witness* (remake of *Our Glass House* with a local charity, the Anah Project); *Off the Curriculum* residencies; Youth Theatre Lab begins<br><br>Cardiff – *Payday Party* to Edinburgh Fringe; *Us Here Now* exhibited at the Senedd; *Epic Fail* and *Posh Club* (with Moving Roots) |
| 2023 | Genocide in Gaza with an estimated 80,000 lives taken between 2023 and 2024; UK government attempts to introduce the 'Rwanda plan' (forced deportations of asylum-seekers to Rwanda); UK government passes Public Order Bill, further limiting rights to peaceful protest | Bradford – *Off the Curriculum*; *Fast, Fast, Slow* (also Blackburn); *Peaceophobia* touring; *Off Road*<br><br>Cardiff – Arts Council of Wales portfolio funding awarded for the first time; *We No Longer Talk*; *Reclaim the Space*; *Demand the Impossible* R&D |

| | | |
|---|---|---|
| 2024 | Labour leader Keir Starmer becomes UK prime minister with a right-wing agenda; far-right riots triggered by online misinformation and anti-migrant rhetoric prompts nationwide anti-racist fightback | Bradford – Performance Collective begins; *In Common* and *Still Waiting* performances; *Public Interest* R&D; the inaugural 29% Festival<br><br>Cardiff – *Demand the Impossible* second R&D; Posh Club (Common/Wealth and Duckie); *Take Your Place* pilot |
| 2025 | Trump re-elected in America; Israel begins siege in West Bank, Palestine | Bradford – *Public Interest* and 29% Festival<br><br>Cardiff – *Demand the Impossible*<br><br>Publish *Do It Yourself: Making Political Theatre!* |

# WORKS-SHOWS

In this section you'll find brief accounts of some of our productions since 2009. We haven't included every show we've made and we haven't just included the shows that received national reviews or created some kind of splash. Instead, we've selected a range of shows that feel important to our development as a company. Taken together, the shows highlight who we are as Common/Wealth, what we want to do and how we want to work. Each show took on a very different form, led by the performers – we try not to get stuck in how we've made something before but reinvent the shape of a show in response to what it needs to be.

Most of the shows here led to some learning that we think it might be useful to share. Some took us in a new direction and others led to important collaborations. As we made this section of the book, it's been great to reflect on shows with our collaborators, including performers and other people who were essential to the process – you'll find their contributions after the main descriptions. Look out for the occasional excerpt from a script or creative exercise along the way.

# THE UPS AND DOWNS OF THE TOWN OF BROWN (2009)

A politically charged musical inspired by Bertolt Brecht and Kurt Weill's opera *The Rise and Fall of the City of Mahagonny*. Staged in a disused courtroom, the show had a 40-strong cast and crew, a full-scale cardboard theatre and 32-piece cardboard orchestra. The play was about shady businesses and a gang of sex workers creating a boomtown, where anything goes if you can afford to pay for it. The world is turned upside down when the Brecht Society shows up, stopping the show mid-flow and sentencing the protagonist to death for not paying the licence fee.

## Seed

Based in a former police station in the boomtown of squatted Bristol, we read Brecht and Weill's *The Rise and Fall of the City of Mahagonny*.

## Context

The fallout from the global financial crisis of 2008 was in full flow, with the bailout of banks and the financial sector and the closing of high streets.

## Site

The Old Magistrates' Court in Bridewell, in the centre of Bristol, was under the guardianship of our friends, the Invisible Circus. The Old Courts were in the centre, containing a courtroom, large foyer and underground police cells (one of which Rhiannon's dad once spent a night in).

## Process

> We denied ourselves nothing. We wrote our own texts – and I also wrote plays – or sliced up other peoples in all directions, then stuck them together differently till they were unrecognisable. We introduced music and film and turned everything top to bottom; we made comedy out of what had originally been tragic, and vice versa. We had our characters

bursting into song at the most uncalled for moments. In short we thoroughly muddled up people's idea of the drama.

Bertolt Brecht[9]

We had no idea about the regulations governing live performance and we believed in everything being free. We don't think we paid for anything, really, except rent on our studio in the same building complex, which was about £20 a month each with four of us sharing. We wanted to perform *The Rise and Fall of the City of Mahagonny* as a complete piece until we learned about the money you need to pay the Brecht Society to put on a Brecht play. We'd have to pay, we wouldn't be allowed to alter the text and we'd need a 32-piece orchestra. Shocked that our political theatre hero would have his work gatekept in this way, we made a pastiche of the original, which explored how the biggest crime is to not be able to afford to pay. We planned to send the script anonymously to the Brecht Society as a protest, but we never did.

## Who

There were so many artists, musicians and performers involved in this show – we honestly can't remember them all. If you were part of this show and are not named here, we're so sorry.

Evie Manning, Rhiannon White, Dougy Francisco, Delroy, Heidi Borg, Sarah Fielding, Naomi Smyth, Coco Banks, Michelle Wren, Nicola Wren, Emma Grant, Justin Squire, Rowan Fae, Eamon, Jassen, Ruari and Oli from the Circus of Invention and two sound artists, Phullopium Dude and Katapulto.

---

[9] Bertolt Brecht, quoted in John Willett (ed., trans.), *Brecht on Theatre: The Development of an Aesthetic* (London: Methuen, 1978), p. 65.

# OUR GLASS HOUSE (2012)

A site-specific performance staged in empty houses, exploring domestic violence. Audiences chose their own journeys around the house, coming together after the performance in the living room to share their experiences. Five characters each occupied their own room: a pregnant woman, a woman who speaks Punjabi and Urdu, an older upper-class woman, a teenage girl and a man. A 10-year-old boy roamed around the house. Performances in the rooms sometimes happened simultaneously, at other times individually. In the final moments, action spilled into the street, with the pregnant woman's refusal to be with a man who hits her – a call to action shared with neighbours and passers-by.

## Seed

An ambulance was called to the house next door. Evie's neighbour had been beaten by her husband and was taken to hospital. The violence had been going on for a long time without anyone knowing. Evie called Rhiannon with the idea to do a show in a residential house, drawing on the promenade, immersive style we'd been working with in Bristol. We'd been friends for years, but Rhiannon hadn't shared that her own life had been affected by domestic violence. We decided to make a show that tackled the hidden nature of domestic violence and initiated street-level conversations about what it means to stay in abusive relationships, how people muster the courage to leave and the role of communities as witnesses.

## Context

The National Centre for Domestic Violence estimates that one in four women in the UK experience domestic abuse in their lifetime, a statistic that is likely to underestimate actual prevalence due to under-reporting. When we made the show, women's refuges in the UK, a lifeline for many, were under threat from austerity-related cutbacks. The show was part of the campaign to protect essential services.

## Site

Staged in residential houses, from council houses to a £3 million house in London. In each site we knocked on neighbours' doors to tell them what we planned to do, checking they were happy for us to be there. Local people helped clean, paint and wallpaper. Working with small budgets, we often lived in the houses we were working in. Being in close proximity to the community helped us deepen the conversations.

## Process

We began with a series of questions that we asked Rhiannon's mum, testing if they were answerable on an emotional level, and whether they would provide the things we needed to create a show. Domestic violence organisations came on board and found more people to interview. We trained to be Freedom Programme Facilitators (freedomprogramme.co.uk), deepening our understanding and enhancing our ability to have conversations with those who had experienced domestic violence.

The women we interviewed were so generous and we wanted to offer something in exchange. We took them on a residential in partnership with a brilliant local charity, Imayla. Inviting them to the first sharing of *Our Glass House*, we made it clear that they could watch what they wanted, leave as they needed and feed back as much or as little as they liked.

Working with professional actors meant that we could draw on verbatim material from interviews without asking anyone to relive their trauma on stage. Some actors worked across the lifetime of *Our Glass House*; other roles were cast anew in each site, so that audiences could hear the story in a local accent. During rehearsals, we worked collectively to discover the moments that would be shared (a movement piece, a dinner scene, a card game) and the moments that told a story (the young girl being ducked underwater in the bath, the rave scene, the pregnant woman climbing out of the window).

# Who

Creators: Evie Manning and Rhiannon White
Writers: Aisha Zia and the company
Composer/Sound designer: Wojciech Rusin
Production design: Michelle Wren, Russ Henry, Tim Mileusnic,
    Emma Byron, Trevor Houghton, Coco Banks
Production management: Rhiannon White
Producer: Evie Manning
Performers: Liz Simmons, Balvinder Sopal, James Lewis, Rew Lowe,
    Dan Hart, Cynthia Whelan, Corinna Marlowe, Jo Cameron
    Brown, Joy Dowle, Kirsty Armstrong, Jasmin Riggins, Cerise
    Reid, Jaden Bardouille, Kyran Jobson, Luke Gordon, Harley
    Kierans

Awarded a Special Commendation by Amnesty International and named 'Pick of the Fringe' by *The Metro*.

## Performing verbatim material
## Balvinder Sopal – performer, *Our Glass House*

I played the part of Sufiya in the original production. I was attracted to the idea of making a show about an issue as important as domestic abuse, especially a show founded on the idea that domestic abuse affects people from all backgrounds. The company was looking for a performer who could speak other languages and I brought Punjabi, Hindi and Urdu to the work.

It was a challenging process, but not the sort you shy away from. The character I played represented women who can't speak English. How the bloody hell do you communicate to someone that this is what is happening on a daily basis? It's hard enough to say you're being abused in English.

We didn't glorify. We didn't exploit people's stories to get funding. It wasn't about that. The production budget was extremely small. I moved over to Bristol for the rehearsal period and I was living in a house that didn't have a cooker or a bath. The conditions were not plush! But I wanted to make work that would speak to many different people and could make a difference. It was about getting the story out there. People were coming to see the show that you would never see in a theatre building.

We were given a house on an estate and people from the local community came and helped build the set. We weren't using someone's street to create art – we were saying, come on, let's create together, let's have an experience and work out the change that might be necessary for this area. Let's do it together. Different groups of people that you would never imagine coming together to watch a show that was meant for everybody.

We were very careful with the testimonies. Sufiya's text was an amalgamation of several testimonies that the company gleaned from interviews. It was verbatim, but it was also a collective voice. We wanted to do justice to the words. Because you're saying people's words, those words carry extra weight and require extra care. There was licence to shift a few things about but we didn't embellish anything. When we were in Bradford, we experimented with getting Sufiya to scream and shout, to rage at the situation, and then leave. But that didn't sit right. She had been so quietly defiant. It didn't warrant the blast at the end for dramatic effect. Instead, the ending became almost prayer-like. She found the strength in prayer to leave and that was fitting because faith was important to her.

In one performance, there was an older gentleman, a Muslim man with a skullcap, who followed her story everywhere. At the end, Sufiya says 'God, give me the strength to live this life, for me, and for my children'. And she says 'amin', and every time she said 'amin', he said 'amin'. There was another moment when a group of Muslim women from a local women's refuge were crying in the middle of one of Sufiya's speeches. I stopped performing. There was a moment of pause, while we all shared the space. I carried on. It felt like that was honouring the words of the people we were performing, as well the experiences of the spectators.

We were sitting in those words and allowing those words. It wasn't about dramatic gesture. As actors, we're always excavating and exploring. But here it was important to just say the words. To allow space for the words to breathe. It was about catching those moments, the realness of it, rather than going for effect. I find it incredibly moving to think about, still. It transcended performance.

At the end there was no curtain call. Instead, the company provided a holding space for people to talk about what they saw and appreciate the stories that were shared. And many nights, women spoke up for the first time about the fact that they were survivors, having never had the power or strength to speak about it before in public.

There's so much work now that uses verbatim material. What Common/Wealth do that is different is keep it in the community. It's theatre at grassroots level. It's about empowering people. It's about saying 'here's the mirror, here's the story'. We want you to experience it with us. And tell us where we're going wrong. Tell us what we can do to make it more honest and real for you.

For anyone out there interested in performing in this way, I'd say know why you're doing it. What does it mean to you to create work like this? If you're in it to make solid change, to change yourself, and understand the world we live in and if you are willing to educate yourself and put that back out into the world, then, absolutely, go for it. Come with your whole self. Don't come with preconceived ideas. Be willing to collaborate. It's about giving. You are there to honour the stories. Know also that it's not about you. You're just the vessel for the story. Take ego out of it and honour the work.

14 *Our Glass House*, London, 2013. Credit: Kalpesh Lathigra

15 *Our Glass House*, Edinburgh, 2013. Credit: Robert Ormerod

16 *Our Glass House*, Edinburgh, 2013. Credit: Robert Ormerod

# NO GUTS, NO HEART, NO GLORY (2014)

A performance in boxing gyms performed by five young women, with the audience on their feet, moving around with the action.

## Seed

Alaa, another neighbour on Evie's street (not the same one as *Our Glass House*), was a boxer. She had nine children and wore niqab. We then found out that there were two Muslim female boxing champions in Bradford, Ambreen Sadiq and Saira Tabasum.

## Context

When we first thought about making the show in 2013–2014, the public narrative around Muslim women was that they were either submissive and controlled by men or running away to join ISIS. The show shook up these stereotypes. It was a chance for young Muslim women to represent themselves, dance, box, swear, get angry, enjoy themselves and be champions. Nowadays it's more common to see images of girls playing sport, and there have been historic developments, such as FIFA, the world governing body for football, allowing players to wear hijabs. But when we made the show, the idea of young Muslim women boxing was literally newsworthy. The show featured in every mainstream newspaper.

During rehearsals, Israel started a new military incursion in Gaza. One of the actors started attending anti-war protests, coming to rehearsals with questions. The journey of her character was about standing up to bullies and we transposed this to become about bullying between nations and standing up for what you believe in.

## Site

Boxing gyms. In the early stages we worked at Huggy's Gym in Bradford, getting on well with Huggy, a bare-knuckle fighter with a big reputation. We were due to open in Bradford on a Thursday. On the Tuesday we got a phone call from a man who said *he* was the owner of the gym, not Huggy. He did not give permission for the show to take place and would call the police if we tried to stage it. Cutting a long story short, we found another venue, but BIG LESSON: always get a contract with the OWNER. Find a site and fall in love, but formalise something on paper.

## Process

We watched boxing lessons, soaking up the energy, discipline and banter. We came up with an emotional score and interviewed female boxers. We delivered workshops with young women in schools and held an open audition, quickly realising that there weren't many actors who were the right fit and that the girls from the schools brought the energy we needed. We went back to schools to run auditions, going on to lead an R&D with the young women who became the cast. After the R&D, the performers started regular boxing training with Ambreen Sadiq and we carried on working, with this experimental phase introducing the cast to the idea that a show doesn't have to be anything like a regular play.

Touring nationally and internationally reinforced our commitment to the 'common why' of the show. In Helsinki there had been a 'hate march' against migrants the weekend before, attended by 10,000 people. In Perth, Australia, we worked with Indigenous young people who faced systematic racism on a daily basis.

The run up to the Edinburgh Fringe coincided with Ramadan, and so we paced rehearsals to accommodate fasting. The gym we used for the Edinburgh performances was on a council estate, attended by young white men and run by their mums. We invited them to the dress rehearsal and waited to see what they made of it. A few cried and one said, 'I felt like I was watching myself up there'. White Scottish boy boxers connecting with Muslim girl boxers from Bradford. The beauty of *No Guts, No Heart, No Glory* was that it was specific to its people and place – young women in Bradford – but connected with people of all ages, genders, identities and nationalities.

## Who

Performers: Seherish Mahmood, Freyaa Ali, Mariam Rashid, Nayab Din, Saira Tabasum
Writer and co-creator: Aisha Zia
Director: Evie Manning
Associate director: Rhiannon White
Boxing coach and script consultant: Ambreen Sadiq
Choreography: Imogen Knight
Composer/Sound design: Wojciech Rusin
Production design: Alice Hoult

Scotsman Fringe First Award, 2014.

Broadcast live on BBC as part of the 'On Stage: Live from Television Centre' collaboration between Arts Council England and Battersea Arts Centre.

*No Guts, No Heart, No Glory* was a co-production with Contact, Manchester.

## Making performance collectively
## Seherish Mahmood, performer

I had seen *Our Glass House* in a council house in Bradford when I was 15. It was the first time I'd seen anything site-specific. A few months later, Evie asked if I could come to an audition and I thought, why not? The R&D went well and I thought that was the end of it because it was dependent on funding. And then Evie got in touch and said, 'We're going ahead and we're going to tour. Are you up for it?' I decided to take a gap year for the tour instead of going to university. I got whisked away, in the best way.

The process was so deep and long. We were training how to be a boxer for an hour, and then going back to working on the script. We were all very different and had different experiences of growing up in Bradford, and we took from each other's experiences. It was a group of girls sitting in a circle and just discussing. We'd have the phone recorder on and it would go from there. We would have prompts – a time where you felt really brave, or a time where you felt really scared. If you were to say what you really wanted to say, what would you say? We also had one-to-one conversations with the writer, Aisha.

At one point we sat down and agreed that we all had an equal role in making the show. No one's the lead and we're not telling one person's story. That was a pivotal point in the whole process. We also spoke with Ambreen, the national boxing champion, about how it was for her growing up as a Muslim woman who ventured into boxing and all the highs and the lows of that. That all went into the play too. I don't think anything was manufactured in any way.

Our characters aligned with who we were. Once we'd decided it'd be equal, everything we did, right down to the way the lights would be, or the music, perfectly reflected who we were. I had a little angry, intense moment, then a bit more of a reflective moment. Someone else had a passionate monologue. There wasn't a complete distinction between the role and each of us. We were versions of ourselves.

At the time, I hated the boxing – it was quite tough, but it was fun to learn how to do it. How to keep your stance and how to throw a punch. 'Can you do a monologue as well please?!' It was about figuring out when you should be taking pauses with your words, how slow you should be, how loud you should be. We trained at a local gym and that's also where we did our rehearsals. The guys would come in and do their own training while we were running around reading our lines. We'd see something happening in the gym and think, 'Oh, that should be in the show'.

We talked about what it was like being young Muslim women but we also talked about the fact that, actually, there's nothing to talk about. We're just living our lives – we hang out with our friends, we come home, our parents are super proud of us doing this show. That was part of what the show was about – breaking those stereotypes down. We were just having a good time and that was part of the defiance.

In Bradford, these stories aren't new and everybody's felt a bit of what we shared. But I was nervous about the Bradford audience the most. You don't know if you'll see someone you know, and theatre wasn't something that people really went to or felt they could go to. We were blown away by the response. The comments that we got from fathers with young daughters, grandmothers, young girls who just started high school. Everyone had something really lovely to say and took something away that I wouldn't have expected.

Taking the show on tour was surreal. I thought, who's going to relate to this? I was very surprised when I saw tears in the audience's eyes and I wish I could have asked what part of it resonated. What got you? It still sticks with me, the range of people that it affected. I didn't expect others to see themselves in it. Normally, you feel that there's a complete disconnect between the experiences of South Asian women and everyone else. It was nice that people felt it was a bit of a mirror.

The experience taught me a lot. It chucked me in at the deep end and it informed everything that I do now. Having a reason for doing what you're doing. Thinking about things in a community sense. If I'm going to earn money, what do I want to be doing, and what can it do for people? That doesn't necessarily have to be performing or theatre. The way that the company listen and the grace they approach things with. I'll always come back to that way of working. To stop and look and say 'Is there art in this? Is there politics in this? What does it really mean?' It's about being a part of something that's bigger than you.

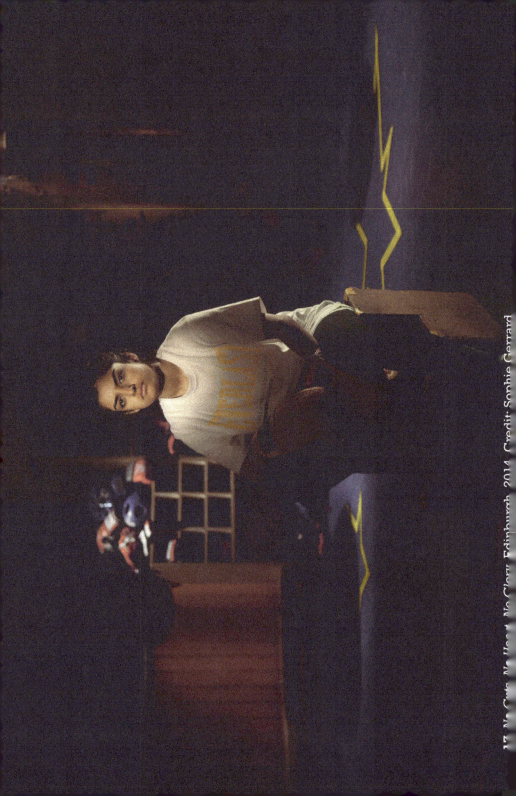

18 *No Guts, No Heart, No Glory*, Edinburgh, 2014. Credit: Sophie Gerrard

# THE DEAL VERSUS
# THE PEOPLE (2015)

*The Deal Versus the People* explored an international trade deal that, if it had come to fruition, would have given corporations more power than elected governments. We worked with people from Bradford not normally represented in politics to create a site-specific event in Bradford City Hall.

## Seed

We were invited by the Trade Justice Movement to make a show about the Transatlantic Trade Investment Partnership (TTIP). A precursor to Brexit, TTIP was a proposed trade deal between America and Europe that would have seen a reduction in food and manufacturing standards (chlorinated chicken, anyone?), worker's rights and privacy.

## Context

We made the show in 2015 at the height of the TTIP negotiations, when there was increasing national press interest. We were galvanised by how little anyone knew about it.

## Site

The council chambers at Bradford City Hall – working chambers where councillors meet and debate. We worked around their schedule and they worked around our set and rig.

## Process

We cast 10 people with experience of unemployment who felt under-represented by formal politics. Four became the core cast with the rest forming a community cast. We met politicians, trade campaigners and civil servants, receiving a whirlwind education on TTIP, which blew our minds. We also started a public campaign called 'We're not stupid', creating pressure around the idea that ordinary people should have a say in decisions that govern their lives.

The show was about power – how much do citizens have, what does it feel like to live without it and how might we get those in power to listen. We staged a playful 'occupation' of City Hall and made a video letter to send to the European Parliament. Fiona made a 'bomb' out of items from the food bank, Cain threatened to set himself on fire on the council table, Wahida got everyone in the audience to put a balaclava on and drum pots and pans, and Tyrell led us in a chant:

It's not just us.

It's all round the world

In Mexico, Indigenous people have taken back their land.

In London, people are resisting eviction from social housing that's been sold off.

In Spain, there's a town that owns all its industry and shares the money equally.

It's not just us.

It's last night's audience

And tomorrow's audience

It's not just us.

But even if it is.

If everyone here fights for an hour, between us we've fought for a month.

If everyone here fights for a month, between us we've fought for a decade.

If everyone here fights for a year, between us we've fought for a lifetime.

There are more people than there are governments.

There are more people than there are corporations.

It's not just us.

It's not just us.

It's not just us.

It's not just us.

It's not just us.

It's not just us.

## Who

Performers: Fiona Broadfoot, Wahida Kosser, Tyrrell Vanzie, Cain Connelly, Trelise Stewart, Haris Ahmed, Barsa Ray, Vanessa Ndukuba, Antony Stevenson, Sharon Grace
Directors: Evie Manning and Rhiannon White
Writers: Aisha Zia and Daniel Bye
Set designer: Michelle Wren
Sound designer: Wojciech Rusin
Digital designer: Matt Wright
Lighting designer: Jacob Gough
Trade Justice Movement consultant: Ruth Bergan

19 *The Deal Versus the People*, Bradford, 2015. Credit: Christopher Nunn

20 *The Deal Versus the People*, Bradford, 2015. Credit: Christopher Nunn

# WE'RE STILL HERE
## (2017)

A site-specific show inspired by the Save Our Steel campaign in Port Talbot. The story was told by a cast of five male actors – four professional and one taking a sabbatical from his steelworker job – alongside a community cast and four teenage performers.

## Seed

We were asked, 'If you were to make a show about contemporary Wales, what would it be?' We were obsessed with Welsh stories of everyday, working class people changing the world – the likes of Aneurin Bevan and Keir Hardie (who was once MP for Merthyr). Where were those leaders in 2017? In Port Talbot the steelworkers were fighting once again against the threat of closure of the steelworks. People were marching and protesting weekly and we thought, there they are, our working class leaders. It felt like the story we needed to tell was happening there and then.

## Context

Tata Steel, the owners of the steelworks at Port Talbot, had announced 750 job losses and closure in the near future. Port Talbot is a town defined by the steelworks. The closure of the works would have a devastating impact on the town and also on Wales. Tata's decision to put the plant up for sale, to put the sale on hold and to offer a deal should workers accept pension reform, all occurred as we were making the show. We were responding to an unfolding story.

## Site

We discovered the old Byass works from walking about. A gang of kids on bikes using the site as their playground showed us around. It was all old industrial structures, moving cogs and ladders. We researched old ghost stories connected to industrial accidents there and, going back for another visit, discovered a working yard and met the yard owner, John – a staunch Welsh republican, Brexit-voting Conservative. We made friends and John became our advocate.

## Process

We interviewed people related to the steelworks: workers, union reps, management and community members. We attended the steelworkers' panto, eventually casting Sam Coombes, steelworker and star of the panto, in the play. We met Gary, the vice-chair of the union and a socialist who believed in people's right to work and a decent pension. Weekly meetings with a group of local people helped us find out more about what was happening in the town. They sense-checked material as it emerged and formed the basis of our community cast. Rehearsals were often attended by steelworkers, watching scenes and giving feedback on what people from Port Talbot would say and do.

## Who

Directors: Evie Manning and Rhiannon White
Writer: Rachel Trezise
Composer/Sound design: Wojciech Rusin
Designer: Russ Henry
Lighting designer: Andy Purves
Movement director: Vicki Manderson
Costume designer: Llinos Griffiths
Casting director: Sarah Hughes
Emerging director: Siobhan Lynn Brennan
Community associate: Nicole Moran
Performers: Sam Coombes, Ioan Hefin, Jason May, Simon Nehan, Siôn Tudor Owen, Callum Bailey, Joseph Reynolds, Isabelle Coombs, Dylan John

*We're Still Here* was a co-production between Common/Wealth and National Theatre Wales.

## *We're Still Here* – script excerpt

XANDER In Port Talbot, South Wales, it's late in the evening, the clear sky a strange amethyst colour. The lights of the steelworks blaze bright against the dusk for tens of miles around. Perhaps it's the bright lights that keep the ghosts away, though they fail to discourage the occasional fox or feral cat drawn by the heat to the plant, fur acquiring over time a new coat of cardinal red; dust from the iron ore. Inside the night workers are beginning their shift, supplying the blast furnace with coke and limestone. They are just a couple of the members of the 4,000-strong permanent workforce remaining to date at these works. They are fathers and mothers and daughters and sons. They are wives and husbands. They are neighbours, with skills and wisdom that the closure of industry cannot take away. In their heads they carry knowledge, in their hands their craft. In their hearts they carry love. From their mouths comes their voice.

Presently, these steelworks are one of only two sites in the UK with a lit blast furnace. These works are the site of the last heavy industry in Wales.

These works are the last bastion; the last outpost, a fortress defending a way of life and a community threatened by the relentless march of global capitalism. These works are the last bastion.

## Making with people
## Jane Slee and Gary Owen – community cast members, *We're Still Here*

*Jane Slee and Gary Owen were members of the community cast of* We're Still Here. *The conversations with Gary and Jane (which led to their contributions here) took place a couple of weeks after Tata's announcement in 2024 that the second of the two blast furnaces at the steelworks was to close, with 2,000 more workers to be made redundant.*

# Jane Slee

My sister-in-law said, 'I've seen something on Facebook – they're looking to talk to people involved in Save Our Steel, something to do with theatre'. Now, I love theatre. My late husband, Gareth, worked in Tata, and had not long been made redundant. He'd been at the steelworks since he was 17 years old and knew it inside out. Gareth had epilepsy, so he couldn't drive. At the first meeting, when they spoke to me, I said, 'Don't talk to me, I'm only the taxi driver'. But then they said, 'Come on. Join in this. Join in that.' And before I know it, I'm in it as well.

The whole experience was so real to what we were experiencing. We were all different ages, different backgrounds. Some still working in Tata, others made redundant. We met new people and reunited with others we'd not seen for ages. We rekindled friendships. Since redundancy, Gareth had stayed in touch with some of the blokes for a while, but when they're still working and he's not, that's difficult. He had experienced some mental health struggles and the show helped put things into perspective. I think it helped him see an end to it, to lay it to rest.

I'm used to theatres with nice plush, red velvet seats. As a young adult I was in the local little theatre where people auditioned for a role, followed a script, sat in a seat, performed on a stage. A very long time ago, my mother loved musicals, so I'd go to musicals. The big London-type shows. *We're Still Here* was very different from all of that – it was a kind of promenade theatre where people were in and out, and it had numerous stages. And it actually did something. Since then, I've been to more theatre like that.

Back then, the show was an eye-opener, both to the steelworks and the way people felt in there. It made us see that, okay, people outside Port Talbot are realising what is going on, and you didn't feel quite so isolated. Maybe they would pick up on a little bit of news and think, I'm going have a little look into that. Find out a bit more. The show got on all the local news and attracted attention to the town. The whole process helped to put us on the map for some people.

At the time, journalists were coming here from out of town, and they had no idea. It felt very much like we were being judged. They didn't know us and they didn't spend any time here. With *We're Still Here*, it was local and the team listened to us. We were given the original script and you could see the elements that moved on because the team listened to us. It became truer to what we know, what we experienced, how we felt. In the original script, one of the characters was afraid of not being able to afford to buy a pram, but we changed that to being worried about not being able to stay in Port Talbot. That was more important to us than being able to buy a pram. Because if he was in Port Talbot, his neighbour would lend him a pram, or someone down the street would lend him a pram. The pram wouldn't have been a problem.

We're a bit of an old-fashioned town, hung up on steel. There were redundancies then and we're back with redundancies now. Right now, you go up town, pubs are empty, restaurants are closing two or three nights a week, because people are not sure what's going to happen. You think, could we have protested more? What could we have done better? Marching and campaigning, but once you're dealing with something as big as Tata, it's a done decision. I don't think whatever we do will change what they've got planned. I think some of us feel a bit defeated.

Whether it's Tata, Corus, British Steel, the Steel Company of Wales, all of them, they have been good and fair many times, but there are times when it feels, 'Nah, that isn't right'. They sponsor a lot of stuff around town – kids football, a half marathon. They try and do stuff, but do they do enough?

It was surprising to have something as contemporary as *We're Still Here* in Port Talbot. The whole experience was surprising considering I was only there to drop Gareth off – that I got into it kicking and screaming 'I'm only the taxi driver!' I was surprised that local people were such good actors. How down to earth some of the professional actors were. How much fun it was. How much I enjoyed it. The venue. We'd been down to the old Byass works for a walk shortly before the show and I said, 'How can you make this here?' My brain couldn't get around it. But when we saw what they'd done to make it safe but still have that industrial feel, the lighting and the sound, it was fabulous.

If someone else was thinking of doing something like this in a town like ours, I'd say join in, have fun, you'll learn, you'll gain, the whole experience will make you think, and even change your opinions on some things. Make sure there is a reduced ticket price for local people. Don't make it mysterious. Don't create any pressure. Give people a chance to be heard – and then listen. Make it with the people. Let them say what they think is important. Trust each other. Understand that everyone has commitments – if someone's working Monday to Friday, they may not be able to commit every night. I work shifts. You can come this night, great. Can't come that night, that's okay.

We're still here. Yma o Hyd. You can get rid of our steel town, we can kick up a fuss. We might get on the news, but I don't think we're big enough to really change the decision that's been made. But we're still going to be here. Still fighting. I'm still here. Here I am. So many things have happened over the years, we've lost so much industry. But we're still here. No matter what you throw at us. We're still here, from Port Talbot, being Welsh, a political thorn in England's side, and we're not going anywhere.

## Gary Owen

I heard about it from the 'Steelworkers R Us' Facebook page. I thought, I'll give it a go. There was a meeting in the St Paul's Community Centre with warm-up exercises and stuff. That was strange. It took me back to being seven years old in a vest and pants, pretending to be a rabbit on the floor. We were all doing this daft stuff.

There was a family feel in a short space of time. A very good vibe. You know when you throw a jigsaw on the table and 30 pieces sort of stick together on their own. There was a good mix between the professional actors and us amateurs, and people worked together so easily. It's a Welsh thing – the Welsh are easy to get on with; they have this energy, this Celtic energy, and it was there with *We're Still Here*.

It was like a play group again, that sort of vibe, and it was fantastic. Imagine throwing 20 lunatics into a room with lots of beer and making them do shit they've never done before. It was like herding cats at one point, and all these cats ended up pointing in the same direction.

The artistic team did an amazing job at motivating people. They really could motivate people. Do they always get this level of motivation from people? Do they put something in water to make them more compliant? We would have done anything to make the show work. 'Go over there and just hover', they said. And we were like, 'Okay, I'll give it a try now'!

I shared a story in the show about my father coming home from the steelworks when I was a kid. My mother would wash his shirt in the sink and hold it up to the kitchen light. I remember the holes burned through it where sparks had caught him. When he washed in the kitchen sink, stripped to his waist, getting ready to go to the club for a pint, there were burn marks on his back. No PPE in those days. Some nights I'd do the story pretty much verbatim, and some nights I'd tangent and start talking about something else, or tell it slightly differently. The freedom of that was lovely.

I performed one of my own songs a cappella. I walked out to the crowd and people were still talking and things going on and noise and all of a sudden it went dark and there's me up on a mound, singing. The song was about the furnace explosion at the steelworks in 2001. Bricks fell onto my mate's car and its roof caved in. I went into this bubble for months and months and months. I just couldn't process it. I won't go into details out of respect for the people who are not here, but I witnessed some horrible things that night.

On 25 November 2024 I'm out of there. It's been 37 years since I started working there. The place is silent. It's switching off, going to darkness, a desolate moonscape. It's eerie. A big ship being slapped about by the sea and pounded by rain. They've taken us off shifts and put us on days in a workshop in the middle of the works. No facilities, 40-hour week, Monday to Friday, then I take redundancy money and leave. It used to be when someone left or retired there was a bit of a collection, buy them some crap, that sort of thing. But now it's like, 'Okay, ta-ra, empty your desk'. The stink of it.

When I think about *We're Still Here* now, it's like life mirroring art or art mirroring life. It told the real story and there were grains of truth all the way through it. Then it was, yeah, we're still here. But now we're not. The camaraderie, that was one of the words in the script, that's gone. Guys who have worked together for years are arguing among themselves because one's staying on and the other one's got to go.

If you made the show now, it would have to be different, a lot darker. You had bits of darkness in *We're Still Here*, but they were instantly lightened. It was a good combination, I thought. There are no shades of light now. The business community here hasn't felt it yet. I've got a couple of friends of mine that run Asian restaurants. They do a couple of grand on a Friday or Saturday night, depending what shift is on. They won't be there. Pub landlords are starting to feel it but there's a mental music scene going on here at the moment. Bands will show up anywhere and plug in and play. They don't need trimmings, fancy lights, smoke machines or proper venues. That's a big plus.

We've done all the marching. All the rah rah rah up on a podium, the local MP and all that. Politicians – I don't trust any of them. You know when an animal is dead. You can trust it. It's not going to harm you and it's not going to bite you. It's not going to claw you to death. Politicians, you can't trust. Even when there's no pulse, no actual signs of life, you cannot trust them.

I was standing in the workshop last week with my mate. We've known each other for more than 30 years. He's a welder by trade, I'm a fitter by trade and we work together as part of a team. I texted him later that day and said, 'Think of all the times we've spent in that workshop and that's probably the last time we'll ever stand at the spot'. He sent me a heart emoji. Because he's my brother. Tears. I'm choking up now. I've literally spent hundreds of hours in there with him, we've made shit and got shit done, had little breaks and cups of tea on exactly that same spot. We come from a time in there when there was brotherhood.

I smile every time I read the words 'We're still here'. I grin, I do. I had the biggest grin for a fortnight. It was fun. It was a fantastic gig. I enjoyed it. There was one or two people in there, local characters; every time I see one of them, I get big hugs off them, big bloke hugs. It felt like a festival. There were little different shows, all bolted together with other little shows surrounded by amusement arcades and lights and smoke machines and candy floss. That's what it felt like, a festival. Get in, get us in your face, get out, get it done, with people standing around outside saying what was that, shocked, like rabbits in the headlights. Watch a band, watch another band, and people are like, what's going on over there, aspects are changing, lights are changing.

The audiences from Port Talbot didn't have a clue. They didn't know what was coming next, because there was something bonkers every single time. The fact that it was 3D and they got to walk through things, and around things, and change where they stood. But the sequence of different things, the way it flowed. It really got through to the guys and girls that worked in the steelworks. The ones who had experience of it could really see themselves in the show. Their wives or partners who had never worked there were like, 'Is this real?' They didn't know. 'Is this what it's like?'

Things changed for me after the show. I used to tolerate a lot of people's bullshit. I started finding a bit more, that Welsh phrase, hwyl, a bit more, 'piss off, no'. I started getting a bit more fire, like a teenager again. I didn't care for a bit. I still don't care now about certain things, and I enjoy telling people I don't care either. I found a little bit of confidence.

21 *We're Still Here*, Port Talbot, 2017. Credit: Dimitris Legakis

27. We're Still Here, Port Talbot, 2017. Credit: Ian Pountney

# RADICAL ACTS
## (2018)

*Radical Acts* was a celebration of disobedient action that women have taken to make change in their own lives and throughout history, performed by a cast of 10 women. The audience were seated at tables and engaged in facilitated conversation as well as watching the performance.

## Seed

It was the 100-year anniversary of women getting the vote and we'd been part of conversations with lots of women around the need to continue to fight for change. Our empty shop in Bradford city centre became the meeting point for 'Radical Snacks', a weekly food and performance workshop with women of all ages. We talked about creating happenings, interventions or a show. In the end, we did all three.

## Context

In 2017, the Labour Party, led by Jeremy Corbyn, campaigned in the national election with a transformative left-wing manifesto. Although they lost (by a narrow margin) the campaign created a renewed sense of hope, of momentum for change.

## Site

The Bradford Club – a former gentlemen's club where women were not permitted entry until 1985. A grand, wood-panelled, stained-glass building above a bookies in town. Radical acts as interventions were also staged in different sites, including the train from Bradford to London, City Park, City Hall.

## Process

We researched radical acts created by women from history, locally and globally. Weekly 'Radical Snacks' sessions opened up conversations about radical acts we had undertaken in our own lives. Collaborator and chef Sonia Sandhu would make a radical snack each week for an hour of eating and discussion and an hour of performance-making. Latifa, in her early seventies, spoke about wishing she had married herself, so we created 'The Wedding of the Year' where 38 women got married to themselves. For 'Mums Work Hard' we worked with mums and their kids to create a radical act performed on a commuter train raising awareness about hunger over the school holidays. 'Peaceophobia' responded to 'Punish a Muslim Day' (see 'Timeline'), when the young women from Speakers Corner had spoken about how Islamophobia affects the men in their lives in public-facing jobs on a daily basis. Inspired by how cars play such a big part in Bradford's male identity and working with the Bradford Modified Car Club, we created a car rally protest. Someone we met from the brilliant Southall Black Sisters remarked on how unusual it was that women were leading a movement to support men and how this represented a new generation of progress.

Our final radical act was a performance created over two weeks of rehearsals with the collective of women. With a short timeframe to work in, women became hosts at their tables. We kept the text simple – a structure, not a script, with each woman writing five lines that were revealed at successive stages of the performance. The show was a live art installation with performative and participatory moments that transformed the space, using the architecture of the building for subversive reveals.

## Who

Performed, written and created by: Nazmeen Akhtar, Nasreen Awan, Ali Briggs, Emerald Crankson, Emma Heald, Megan Holdsworth, Queen Latifa, Mariam Nisa, Mussarat Rehman, Paula Trotter, Scout Wormsley
Co-directors: Evie Manning and Rhiannon White
Assistant director: Jaasra Aslam
Movement director: Pauline Mayers
Associate artist and chef: Sonia Sandhu
Set designer: Russ Henry

Costume designer: Rachel Owen
Lighting designer: Andy Purves
Composer and musical director: Mariam Rezaei

## *Radical Acts* writing exercise (age, place, situation, feeling, act)

We created a simple storytelling structure which allowed the performers to each tell a story in a stripped back way, without exposing them too much. The stories were told at different intervals throughout the show:

### Naz
I'm 29 years old
I'm in Bradford College
I went for an interview without any qualifications or anyone with me
I'm absolutely terrified
I made a decision for myself to go against my family and educate myself

### Megan
I'm 18
I'm in my sister's flat in Grimsby
It's my time to choose
There's butterflies in my stomach and nerves shaking my whole body
I choose love

### Mariam
I'm 12
I'm in the assembly hall in St Joseph's Catholic College
We have Catholic Mass every fortnight
My voice and the paper I'm holding are shaking
I read an Arabic prayer out loud
(reads *Surah Fatiha*)

## Nasreen
I'm 36
I'm in my house in Bradford
There's a lot of shouting
My whole body is shaking
I turn around and slam the door

## Emma
I'm 16
I'm in Bradford Interchange
Waiting for a coach to Nottingham
My spine is tingling with excitement
I go to an Another Level concert without telling my parents

## Ali
I'm 35
I'm outside the BBC TV studio in Leeds
I'm on the Piss on Pity demo
I'm angry and nervous
I give the signal to my friend who's blind to bring down her placard on the policeman's head

## Emerald
I'm 28
I'm in a police station in Brixton
They start recording
My heart is beating really fast
I tell them everything

## Latifa
I'm 27
In Bradford, at home
He's outside the door. Jalna is with me.
My body was like jelly
I said no, I call the police

**Mo**
I'm 18
I'm in my mum's living room
There's a man come to view me as a prospect for marriage
I'm feeling rebellious
I don't wash for a week, put oil in my hair, I stink

**Paula**
I'm 35
I'm in a council house in Holmewood
Waiting for him to go to work
My heart is racing
I pack the van, take everything, take the kids and I'm gone before he gets home

23. Radical Acts, Bradford 2018. Credit: Lizzie Coombes

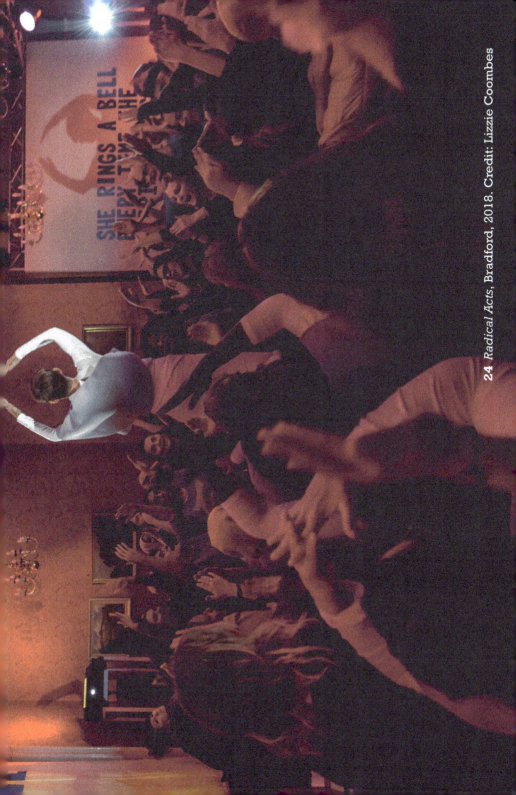

24 *Radical Acts*, Bradford, 2018. Credit: Lizzie Coombes

# I HAVE MET THE ENEMY (AND THE ENEMY IS US) (2019)

*I Have Met the Enemy* was part techno party, part investigation, part call to action. It asked its audiences to take a close look at the UK defence industry and the role it plays in military conflict and occupation around the world.

## Seed

We were approached by the artistic director from Northern Stage who was interested in us making a show about young Muslim girls from the UK going off to join ISIS in Syria. We hated the idea.

## Context

However, we agreed it would be a good idea to make a show about war. The UK is one of the world's biggest arms manufacturers, complicit in fuelling military violence, supporting corrupt and authoritarian governments, and devastating communities across the globe. War was ravaging Syria and conflict continued to rage in Palestine, Yemen, Iraq and Afghanistan, supported by the UK and using weapons designed and built in the UK. Families exiled from their land, traumatised by occupation and war, walking on foot with all they had, sailing on dinghies across the Mediterranean, all while the arms trade profited. We wanted to face up to the arms trade and bring our complicity closer to audiences so they could feel it too.

## Site

We staged the show in communities where the army goes to recruit young people – working class areas with few opportunities. The set featured 72 metronomes with wirelessly controlled light and sound, representing the 72 Eurofighter jets sold to Saudi Arabia by UK-based arms company BAE Systems.

## Process

We met Mo'min Swaitat, a Palestinian performer and artist, at an early R&D. With him, we decided to bring together people who had lived under military occupation and those who had served in war, telling the story through the lens of their experiences. We undertook an open casting process, looking for a soldier, and found Alex Eley, a Welshman who had served in Afghanistan. We also contacted Comra Films in Yemen, casting a third performer to appear in the show via a digital link-up – Shatha Altowai, a Yemeni visual artist. The three performers spent time asking each other questions and their responses formed the basis for the show.

## Who

Performers: Mo'min Swaitat, Alexander Eley, Shatha Altowai
Directors: Evie Manning and Rhiannon White
Dramaturgy and text: Hassan Mahamdallie
Video production: Osama Haji
Production design: Robbie Thomson
Electronics and tech design: Jamie Grier
Sound design: Robbie Thomson and Jamie Grier
Voice actor: Aina Khan

Co-production with Northern Stage.

## Performing from lived experience
Shatha Altowai, Mo'min Swaitat, Alexander Eley – performers, *I Have Met the Enemy (and the enemy is us)*

### Deciding to take part

**Shatha:** I was making art in Yemen when the war erupted. My husband carried on working in the capital, protecting our house, and I moved to a rural area. But I decided to move back. I said that we will die together, rather than I hear about something happening to him in the city. While he was on the road to meet me, our neighbour's house was targeted by air strikes, and our house was destroyed. We became displaced for two years, and we continued making art. I used to take my paints into the cafe, disconnecting myself from the surroundings, even while the earth was shaking from the air strikes. My husband would take his piano and play. The media were curious about our story and filmed a short documentary. We talked about peace and democracy and the authorities were not happy. It was safer to stop making art. So, when I saw the call from Common/Wealth looking for a Yemeni artist with experience of war, I thought, 'I'm not able to make art but now it is time to share my story'.

Was it risky? Nothing is guaranteed in Yemen. The reason my husband and I had to eventually flee to Scotland was because we were talking about peace on the documentary and the authorities didn't want that talk. Because of that, when I took part in the play, I was expecting anything. First, because I am a woman. Second, because I am an artist. I have no regrets.

**Mo'min:** Common/Wealth wanted to do a play on the impact of the arms trade. They wanted people who had personal experience of being impacted by the military. We then found Alex, a British soldier who had recently returned from Afghanistan, and he and I worked together for a period of research and development. It was intense. We found common ground in our love for music and food, and we are a similar age, which helped us. We also had common ground in the sense of understanding being around the military. The tension produced by being surrounded by guns, or using guns, or having guns used against you. We took a week to think about whether to move forward. If we wanted to go ahead, I needed to consider a lot of details, because it is not an easy subject. For me, the British army is colonial history; for him, he's a proud soldier. It needed a lot of understanding from the both of us. There were many obstacles for us both to cross. And then here comes Shatha with a completely new angle, joining us on screen. It was important to have a Yemeni voice, as we were creating the show during a time when British-made military hardware was being used to bomb Yemen on a daily basis.

**Alex:** I was in drug rehab after a period of service in Afghanistan, suffering with PTSD and other mental health issues. A member of staff at the rehab unit showed me the callout from Common/Wealth and I thought, 'I've got nothing to lose'. When you're in rehab, it's all about finding a new perspective on life and not reconnecting with old jobs or interests. I had no experience in acting. I was so open minded at the time. This is what life can be, if you allow it to be. I really felt that. I had no understanding of what to expect. In the audition, I had to do some improvised dance. Soldiers get told to stand still and be rigid, and now I'm in this theatrical environment where everyone is open, really in the now, in flow. I was out of my comfort zone, improvising on the spot, rolling around on the floor. Being in a performance is about really getting out of your own way and allowing the moments to create themselves. I was offered the spot and it felt like continuing recovery for me. It could open something up for me – there was that risk there – and I had a team to support me through the process. Rehab staff, psychotherapist, drug counsellors. I was quite well armed – no pun intended.

## Deciding to share your story

**Shatha:** It was very hard for me to share my experience of living in a war zone. But I felt like the story needed to be told. Yemeni people had shared a lot of information on the news and social media about the hundreds of people being killed. But we rarely had the opportunity to share our stories in an artistic way – in a way that would give a fuller version of our lives affected by war.

**Mo'min:** The very hard thing was making the decision to share my personal story. This was very difficult, this decision. It helped to sit down and talk about what kind of story we wanted to be telling but also *how* to tell it and *where* the story should come in the show. We created holding spaces for each story, so that they each became very important moments for the audience.

There were so many difficult decisions. The working process took a long time. The show was prepared over almost two years so the rehearsal schedule wasn't very intense. We'd have three days a week, four days a week, sometimes five days a week, and then we'd go off for a couple of weeks. In between, you would have time on your own, to go for a long walk, meet friends and family members, process your feelings. We didn't go by the usual theatre schedule of three weeks rehearsal followed by opening the show in the fourth week. Every time, you came back to rehearsals with more material and were more sure that you wanted to share. If it had been a three-week rehearsal period, the show would have fallen apart. It was too intense to hold in three weeks.

We did exercises about everything – what we felt in the morning, what we think, what we like, what we don't like. We spoke about everything. Anything we needed to talk about we sat down and talked about it. We went out for dinner as a group to talk more about the decisions we had made. There was nothing shared in the play that someone was unhappy with.

**Alex:** I came to understand more about my life and my history through working with writer Hassan Mahamdallie during the R&D process. He would ask me about the things that happened out there and he wrote it down and gave me a transcript of everything I'd said. We'd then create a two-minute piece. When we were working on a night-vision scene, I had to stop and go and get some fresh air. I felt guilt about being present in that operation. When you're out there, you can really tap into that adrenalised, masculine, warrior state, but when you're in a reflection process, you have to look again at the people that were there. If someone's not fighting back, they're not a combatant. You can't understand it as war. War is when someone is shooting at you or attacking you. But even then, you have to ask why. They don't want us there. You can dress it up as war, but they just don't want you there. And you're there. That's why it's happening.

## How to tell your story

**Shatha:** I just said what happened. I didn't say anything against anyone. It would have been dangerous for me to do anything more. I just said what happened. I was affected. My house was affected. These are the facts. During the show, I asked Mo'min and Alex to rearrange the room in the performance space as it was in Yemen and invited people into my house. It felt like you had been there, in the house, before it was destroyed.

If we couldn't physically be together, it was really powerful to collaborate through screens. It delivered the same story and that will have an impact. If we couldn't make a big change through the political sphere, at least the ones who are most affected were advocated for. This is what I felt like as Shatha, whose house was destroyed. Knowing people had heard my story and had heard what was happening. Knowing that there are actually some people who know. In the political world, there are so many different views and there is a misuse of information. Nobody actually knows the truth until they hear it from the people directly affected.

**Mo'min:** I was completely against showing my vulnerability even as an actor to British audiences. I had so much to say to British audiences, but I didn't want them to feel that I was a vulnerable actor, with them sort of handing their own vulnerability onto me. I wanted them to be vulnerable.

**Alex:** We were careful to work to the right level of vulnerability and no more. Finding the right way the audience would be able to understand. There was a scene that showed my experience of being in night vision inside a house and seeing women being scared. I was trying to represent the local population and thought a lot about how I could add them in without feeling like I was just talking about myself. I tried to show how we affected people. Telling a story about the fear that we induced every day. What they might be thinking and feeling when they hear the helicopters. When they hear the guided missile launch system going off. People with no electricity waiting in the dark. Imagine that feeling: 'Is this the end for us?' Sitting silently. That tension. We were creating that every day for people. No wonder they wanted to kill us. They tried to put a stop to it. We tried to carry it on.

When it came close to the performance, I had coaching on my breathing and my communication. I am a fast communicator, like a lot of Welsh people. A specialist came in to give us coaching. To breathe. To hold the silence. It was very powerful teaching which I still hold with me today. When you're in performance, no one knows what you're going to say. When you're thinking, 'Oh no, I've forgotten the next part', you can own that and you can really play with the audience. Hold that silence for a bit longer. Choosing to not step into the panic. I needed that for my life. I can just be a human being and hold space. There's no need to fill the gap. The gaps are where the nourishment can be and where the real power can be for people.

## *How to create across distance*

**Shatha:** It was too much of a risk for Common/Wealth to come to Yemen, and because of my nationality as Yemeni, there were no open doors for me to go to the UK. We managed to work together through the internet. We discussed how we were going to shape the story together. I started to tell them about my experience and Alex and Mo'min started to tell me about theirs. We asked each other questions and we formed the whole theatrical experience together. I had to plan everything, because the electricity was unreliable. One time, I had my sister's wedding in a village and we didn't have internet access in that area. I went to a hotel to do our meetings for three days. I had to make myself ready for the wedding and then do the meetings, have the wedding, have a call, go and do everything I have to do for the family, and go back and plan everything that we agreed on for the next day's rehearsal!

Because of the lack of internet in Yemen, I pre-recorded my part in the play. For the recording, I had to count, and imagine myself there, inside the play. I said my part then kept silent for a couple of seconds, imagining Mo'min was asking a question, and then replying. It was a really exciting experience. I didn't know how it was going to end up and I was surprised to see the short videos of myself inside the play. It felt like it was me there. Everyone was hearing my name, and even though I couldn't continue my own artistic practice at the time, I could use art to advocate for people affected by war.

**Mo'min:** I was the one in the show who was having the conversation with Shatha when she was on screen, and I had to be on cue as an actor. I had to bring my tools as an actor and help bring her to life in the space. It was a quiet and gentle moment in the show and this reflected what she wanted to share with the audience. She wanted to show herself as an artist.

**Alex:** I met Mo'min at the audition. It was interesting to meet someone who's got a critical view of the armed forces. I found that really humbling. I understand more now about the history of the British Empire and how we've taken things in the world. I heard that from Mo'min in the first person. As a soldier myself, I stand up for what I believe in, and at the time that was King, Queen and Country and all the stuff that we get taught is good for society. I have different views now. I don't believe that we should be on different lands, imposing our politics on people.

A part of the show was improvised by Mo'min and me every time. It allowed for more cultivation of emotion – it pulled the audience in. When Shatha came in, we gained another perspective. How the arms trade affects people in multiple areas of the world. People who are trying to live their life. The cause of the distress is Britain because, fundamentally, the weapon systems are made here. We showed the policies and the conversations and the financial deals. And then she came on and gave a real account of her life. In Yemen, trying to get on with her work, trying to create in the art space. A space that gets ripped apart by bonds and munitions.

## What others can learn from our experience

**Shatha:** I wish the world would make it easier for artists to move around. We open borders for warlords to go and negotiate but we don't open borders for artists to tell stories and be peacemakers. Artists can transfer a peaceful message.

**Mo'min:** In the theatre, not only in Britain but also in other places, there is a lot of hijacking of cultural narratives by people who have not had relevant experience of what they are making work about. This should be understood very deeply. If you want to do political theatre about British politics, especially foreign politics, you need to invite artists from other cultures to be part of your show from day one of the process. That will bring a lot of value to you, into your work, and into the story. Provoke your audience. British theatre is very gentle, very beautiful. At the Freedom Theatre in Jenin, where I trained, we made theatre for our community, not just theatre that we liked to see, or theatre for the sake of theatre, but theatre to provoke the audience to speak and debate. Freedom Theatre was a factory of argument. Provoke a conversation with the local community and the community in general. Dare and dive deep. There are many obstacles, but I urge you to not care and to do it anyway. You have the grounds, you have the capacity and you have the tools.

**Alex:** When you're making a play about another country, you need to sit with people in that country. It will quickly become apparent that you don't really know what the facts are. If you've got a real calling to make political theatre, you should go and be with the people you are making theatre about. You need to be spending time there – as long a time as possible – to really tune in to the conversation that they are having about their own land. You might see more than you think. You might learn more. That will change the course of your life and change the course of your play.

25. *I Have Met the Enemy*, Bradford, 2019. Credit: Christopher Nunn

26 *I Have Met the Enemy*, Bradford, 2019. Credit: Karol Wyszynski

# PEACEOPHOBIA (2020)

A response to global and local Islamophobia staged in multistorey car parks, made with and performed by three British Muslim Pakistani men from Bradford.

## Seed

At the time of the very first R&D for *Radical Acts*, flyers were being distributed online and in mosques and community spaces promoting 'Punish a Muslim Day', encouraging attacks on Muslim people. The young women from Speakers Corner were shocked and scared for themselves and also for the men in their lives. We planned a radical act car-meet to bring men together to talk about Islamophobia. At the car-meet, Ali, who runs Bradford Modified Car Club, said he'd always wanted to be an actor. We do not have to hear that twice! Each show lays seeds for the next.

## Context

Since 9/11, Islamophobia has become widespread in media and political discourse. In 2020 there was 'Punish A Muslim Day' and in 2024 we saw far-right racist riots fuelled by Islamophobia in the UK. The performers have grown up alongside Islamophobia and, through the play, they share stories of everyday and institutional discrimination.

Before *Peaceophobia*, car-meets were illegal in Bradford, with police regularly breaking them up. We invited the Chief Superintendent of West Yorkshire Police to see the show, and they engaged in conversations with Ali afterwards, agreeing that they wouldn't break up car-meets in future. Since then, Ali has held legit car-meets in all kinds of locations – the football ground, the university – building an understanding of car culture and why it's so important to young men in the city.

Touring alongside *Peaceophobia* is an award-winning photography exhibition, *Sisterhood*, showcasing the women of Speakers Corner. A refrain we hear all too often about this show is, 'What about the Muslim women – where are they?'

A liberal Islamophobic dig that infers Muslim women's visibility is subjugated by men. We reply by saying the women are in the large-scale portraits you just walked through to get to your seat, the women conceived the show, the women shaped the script, the women directed the play – did you not see them?

## Site

Multistorey car parks, which usually don't have walls and have great views, meaning that the cityscape bleeds into the world of the show, and vice versa.

## Process

We attended car-meets, getting to know the car scene, and held our first R&D the weekend before lockdown in 2020. At our second R&D, writer Zia Ahmed brought text and everyone was blown away by how he had infused everyday stories with poetry and rhythm. The actors knew they could change anything they wanted, and they did. More lockdowns, and a year later, we went into rehearsals. Evie, mindful about not allowing her voice to dominate, made sure the Speakers Corner co-directors spoke first when giving notes in rehearsal.

In Bradford our audiences were young, predominantly Muslim, and understood Islamophobia and car culture. We wanted other audiences to see the true beauty and power of Islam, so often denigrated in UK media and politics. The show ends with Casper, wearing a thobe, reciting the call to prayer. His voice resounds out of the car park to the streets outside. It was a claiming of space and narrative.

## Who

Performers: Mohammed Ali Yunis, Casper Ahmed and Sohail Hussain
Writers: Zia Ahmed with Mohammed Ali Yunis, Casper Ahmed and Sohail Hussain

Directors: Maleehah Hussain, Mariyah Kayat, Madeyah Khan,
    Evie Manning, Rosema Nawaz, Iram Rehman and Sajidah
    Shabir
Composition and sound design: Wojciech Rusin
Production design: Rosie Elnile
Lighting design: Andy Purves

Co-produced by Fuel and Common Wealth.

## Performing from lived experience
Casper Ahmed – performer, *Peaceophobia*

One of the first plays I attended, Common/Wealth's *I Have Met the Enemy*, changed my perspective on theatre entirely. I went with a few friends of mine and, I must admit, I was completely lost for the first 10 minutes, quietly thinking to myself, 'This might not be our thing'. The sudden changes in atmosphere took me by surprise. As the lights flickered, the sound of music filled the air, every pair of eyes were fixated on one area. It took me a moment to realise the performance had begun. The story captured narratives of the harsh realities of war. The alternating perspectives of the soldier and those affected by the soldier's actions, took my attention. The cast shared something truly profound and opened my mind to the beauty and possibility of theatre.

I believe that every individual has a backstory which has altered their way of life. No one is a blank canvas. These untold stories are our shared reality. With *Peaceophobia*, only the stories we felt comfortable with sharing made it into the performance. I found myself becoming increasingly at ease over time and was able to share a lot more than I anticipated. Irrespective of how distressing the narrative may be, sharing it can inspire others.

Your willingness to take risks often depends on your recent interactions with others. When I embarked on the journey of *Peaceophobia*, it felt particularly precarious. Initially, my mind raced, filled with worst-case scenarios. However, as I delved deeper into the world of theatre, I began to appreciate the transformative potential it holds.

Through the R&D we developed a good rapport and understanding, and it soon began to feel like home. The young women from Speakers Corner and the three of us performers still see ourselves as a family unit. We established a strong bond and this made it easier for us to share our stories.

Our inaugural performance was nerve-racking. I had never acted before, and I felt an overwhelming urge to flee. The voice in my mind was deafening – 'This isn't me!' But I became at ease when I witnessed the audience's warm reception. After our first performance in Bradford, many audience members approached us to share their own stories. It was a profound moment. I was inspired and encouraged to continue. This is one of the reasons I remain involved with the project till today. It is an incredible honour to witness the impact of *Peaceophobia* in the lives of others.

During the show, I share a deeply spiritual experience, which culminates with me singing the call to prayer at the end of each performance. It embodies a sincere root of gratitude, encompassing both giving and receiving love simultaneously. These moments gently dismantle stigma and prejudice in an alluringly reflective, calm and spiritual manner. People inherently recognise what is peaceful. Such experiences offer a chance to realign both thoughts and spirit.

We had been given a platform to express our outrage at Islamophobia; however, the reactions we received when touring were illuminating. Many audience members shared that they had never encountered this more nuanced side of being Muslim – their understanding had been shaped solely by what they saw on television or other media.

The call to prayer in the play serves the same purpose as anyone listening to it on YouTube. Platforms like YouTube and theatre are art forms that transcend boundaries. Through the tranquil call of prayer, I demonstrate that Islam is a peaceful religion, as it has always been. Despite what challenges the world presents, we continue to embody this spirit of peace.

The time we spent in the rehearsal room assembling the show was truly unique, informal and unorthodox, and we all relished the experience. The project was never viewed as just a job. We were compensated spiritually and ethically while getting the chance to tour and explore different cities. Each moment spent in that rehearsal space channelled warmth and hospitality. There was always laughter, playful behaviour and plenty of good-natured teasing among us. Yet, when the time came for us to focus, we knew how to buckle down and get the work done. We shared jokes, tackled tasks together, supported one another and often enjoyed meals as a team.

As a trio of performers, we realised in the early stages that we could not have independently achieved as much as we did together with Speakers Corner. Speakers Corner were incredibly supportive throughout, offering valuable perspectives and fresh ideas. It truly was a collaborative effort. We would draft a section of the script, only for them to remind us, 'Hold on, we need to also focus on the theatrical vision, and not just car culture aimed at the male audience'.

Some may wonder what it was like collaborating with an organisation predominantly led by white individuals, exploring themes of racism. The group from Speakers Corner, along with the three of us, are Muslims, and all of Asian descent. While Evie could be deemed as the 'odd one', the reality was different. Her kind nature, openness and acceptance embraced us from the start. Aside from a few colleagues from a previous job, I did not hold many positive interactions with white individuals. The entire production team were incredibly welcoming and supportive. They were considerate around our requests to perform daily prayers and ensured that our halal dietary requirements were met. There was a sense of belonging and equality for everyone.

To anyone considering embarking on a similar journey, my advice is simple: be open. Embrace your creativity and allow yourself to share your story. Although this may require you to step outside your comfort zone, be open to the opportunities which await you. I believe sharing experience within theatre is a profound form of art, one that not only helps me but also offers others a different insight. My counsel is to be creative. There is someone in the audience who could benefit from your journey. We do not have the luxury of time to make every mistake ourselves; we should aim to learn from the experiences of others.

Remember: it doesn't have to be a grand narrative. Every story individually holds boundless power. To each unfamiliar face, your story could be a familiar one. Who knows, it could very well shape the future of their story. It truly could.

27 *Peaceophobia*, Manchester, 2021. Credit: Ian Hodgson

28 *Peaceophobia*, Manchester, 2021. Credit: Ian Hodgson

# US HERE NOW | RECLAIM THE SPACE (2022/23)

*Us Here Now* and *Reclaim the Space* celebrated the people of East Cardiff, their stories and their power. At the end of summer 2020, after the first pandemic-related lockdown, artist and photographer Jon Pountney and Common/Wealth worked with people in East Cardiff to capture a snapshot of life in the sunshine. For six months, 12 larger-than-life-sized portraits were exhibited on a 24-metre-long wall near the Tesco supermarket in St Mellons. The community feedback was so positive that the following summer we commissioned a permanent piece of outdoor art from the renowned international street artist Helen Bur. Capturing the heart and soul of St Mellons, *Reclaim the Space* now occupies the wall, featuring over 50 local people having a mass 'lie-in' on the fields behind the supermarket. The artwork shows people of all ages lying on the grass, looking back at the viewer, enjoying the sun, eating, cuddling, playing with their dogs and kids and bikes, breastfeeding, having a nap, reclaiming their space.

## Seed

We had just got an office in East Cardiff when the pandemic struck. We wanted to create something that introduced us to the community, and the community to us. We knew that what was needed the most (through being from there) was to tell a different story. We wanted to challenge the dominant, negative narrative by reminding people of how brilliant, beautiful and powerful they are, especially when they are together. We couldn't make or perform live theatre, so we created a process of meeting outdoors, having chats in the street and capturing people looking and feeling powerful.

## Context

Since it was built, East Cardiff has been maligned by outsiders, including politicians and the media. Jon's photographs asked the viewer to look at East Cardiff afresh. The images challenged perceptions of the everyday and ignited a sense of pride and excitement, generating feelings of optimism for the future.

For people who peddle the negative stereotypes, it challenged preconceptions of the area, confronting notions of danger and 'otherness'.

## Site

St Mellons council estate surrounds a central square which includes a supermarket, doctors' surgery, a pub, chemist and chip shop. This artwork was installed on an abandoned wall opposite the surgery, next to the supermarket. It's a really busy thoroughfare, with many of the community walking this route on a daily basis to reach the shops and school.

## Process

When making *Us Here Now*, we met people outside the shops, on the street, in front and back gardens and on the meadows that had sprung up among the contrasting backdrop of housing estates and rural hills that edge the horizon in this part of Cardiff. We sat with people outside their houses on deck chairs as they painted each other's nails, sat on skate ramps, hung out with Tesco workers on their lunch breaks. We took hundreds of photos and had hundreds of conversations.

Once we had all the photographs, we invited the community to co-curate which we would use, what stories we would tell and what that would feel like for the people who would view the work. We discussed colours, shapes, formation and what would make us feel good. It was a very important process to get right.

*Us Here Now* was only ever temporary, and we treated the wall as we would an exhibition site. When it was taken down, the local community had a strong reaction, and it was hard for people to understand why it had to go. In 2022 we toured the exhibition to the Pierhead Building in Cardiff Bay – a building that sits directly opposite the Senedd (Welsh Government). Here we were in direct conversations with power on how working class communities are viewed, treated and resourced. We invited the community to stand with their portraits and speak directly of their experiences of misrepresentation and the damage it causes.

In response to the requests from the community, we were able to commission an artist to create a new artwork for the wall. Co-curating with our Sounding Board we chose Helen Burr to work with us, responding to the local need and building on the story that needed to be told about the place.

*Reclaim the Space* was an artwork that featured over 50 community members lying on the fields behind Tesco, opposite Cath Cobb woods. Previously the location of the St Mellons festival, which stopped in the 1990s, the woods had become the site of multiple murders and assaults – a no-go area for the community. We photographed people lying on the field, chilling, playing, having picnics. We met so many brilliant people who were keen to be involved and do something positive. One grandmother drove two carloads of her family down to be part of it.

The final artwork was painted over two weeks. The wall is eye-level, and local kids and families sat and watched as Helen painted 50 people onto it by hand. Young girls asked Helen how she got into painting and whether she got paid, perhaps imagining that they could do that too. People brought gifts – beer, wine, food and music. We dedicated the artwork to one of Rhiannon's neighbours, a big personality from the area who had passed away while we were painting.

## Who

*Us Here Now* and *Reclaim the Space* photography: Jon Pountney
Installation: Russ Henry, Hotsoup House

*Reclaim the Space* was commissioned by the Sounding Board, and designed and created by Helen Bur.

## Photography and performance in working class communities
Jon Pountney, *Us Here Now*

*How did Us Here Now come about?*

Common/Wealth came to me and said, 'We can't put anything on because of COVID, but can we do a photography project with you?' So, we spent weeks in St Mellons, Trowbridge, Llanrumney – the whole of East Cardiff – photographing people in their gardens because of social distancing. People know Rhiannon and her sister, who lined up a lot of the portraits, and we got some good material. The photographs were displayed on an abandoned wall in the shopping area. And everyone – us, the community – thought they wouldn't last five minutes. But they were up there for six months and not one scratch on them. Not one bit of graffiti. I was pleasantly surprised. It taught me that the community take ownership of things when they can tell they are done in the right kind of spirit.

*What's the most powerful photo you've taken for Common/Wealth?*

It's a picture of a girl called Ocean drinking from a bottle of lemonade. We took it in St Mellons by the community centre. I saw her drinking, covered in sweat. She had just been part of some fun day, playing basketball, and all the kids were outside eating oranges. She was gazing out at the view, which is very unusual, and then she turned to directly meet my gaze. The picture reminds me of Manet's *Olympia*.

*How do you tell the story of people and place?*

So much photography depicting working class life is people on drugs, burned-out cars, decaying buildings. I like some photography that does that, but I made a conscious decision not to make work like that. A lot of my work is trying to obviate that depiction of working class life. When I document a process, it has always been important to me to show that working class people have nice lives and are doing work that they enjoy. Life, work – it isn't always shit. You can enjoy life, be proud and be part of the working class!

Place is inextricably linked with community. In the Valleys of South Wales, the communities are a certain way because of where they are. People found coal and iron in those areas, they built houses and put people there to take that stuff out of the ground and make it into something. Now, mining has stopped, but the people are still there. It's the same in many working class communities. I think this is why I feel so protective over places like the Valleys in a way that I can't quite put into words.

If you're working with communities, you can be from any class or place. What's important is to spend time in the area first. Spend lots of time. I would say it takes years. It's about being able to talk to people about different things on many levels. You've got to foster a curiosity to engage with people and get to know them. Not to be there in a false way but to make friends. Creative people working in the cultural sector can sometimes forget how otherworldly and strange they appear to others.

*How do you photograph live performances?*

Use photography to document and capture the essence of shows. Taking pictures of performance is quite a mechanical process where you follow what's happening and ensure it's in focus. Rehearsals can be more interesting because you're trying to capture people developing something in the moment. There can be more of a life spark. If it's the performance, you capture and copy what is already made rather than interpret a process.

When you are taking photographs, you have to think of the endpoint. If you're photographing something for promotional purposes, that may limit your use of effects. If it's a poster image, then that's using a different part of your brain again – think about how to tell the story of a play in one image. A good composition doesn't come about in the way you may think it does. It's less about technique and more about trust and intuition. Go with your gut instinct.

*Any advice for other photographers?*

Tell stories about people who are characters. Each person you photograph is special and you're trying to bring their character across, not make them fit a narrative. If you go with that narrative already in your mind, you'll create work that isn't truthful. There's a balance between showing something honest that will hold attention and showing a community in a patronising or othering way. That is a narrow tightrope sometimes for photography. I think that a lot of people get the balance wrong. They can miss the living spark of people or the situation and can so easily depict things in misleading or negative ways. If you're there to document the experience, you've got to understand the experience, not judge it.

Question what is possible. Working with press reps at large cultural organisations to get an image for a production can be difficult. Getting them to understand what they are looking at can be difficult. They've perhaps been more used to working in middle class spaces. Sometimes, they don't even appear to want to know about the communities they work in and struggle to come to terms with the menu in the local cafes. I've been in situations where press reps can miss the essence when they look at a photograph.

Keep learning. You can't ever go in and think, I've done 10 of these now, and I know exactly what I'm doing. The next one will always teach you something new.

29 *Us Here Now*, Cardiff, 2020. Credit: Camilla Brueton

*Reclaim the Space*, Cardiff, 2023. Credit: Jon Pountney

# OFF ROAD (2023)

*Off Road* aimed to rewrite narratives around perceived antisocial behaviour, tackling the stigma around quad bike and motorbike culture and sharing the other side of the story about police encounters and Bradford postcode rivalry. Created with young people and rap artists from Windhill, Wrose and across Bradford, and commissioned by Bradford Youth Service, *Off Road* continues to be performed as part of training events and in schools, opening up dialogues about what it's like to grow up in Bradford.

## Seed

Fakhera Rehman, ward officer for Shipley from Bradford Council, approached us after watching *Peaceophobia*. She was having conversations with local residents about young people and off-road vehicles (quad bikes and scooters) and wanted a creative intervention to open dialogue with young people and the community.

## Context

*Off Road* started out exploring the culture of off-road vehicles in a small area of our city and ended up highlighting thousands of young people struggling and vilified by the community and in the media. Their stories showed that they were aware of how they were viewed as violent, dangerous, antisocial nuisances. They positioned this against their reality: not a lot to do, not a lot of support and relationships between young people and services at an all-time low. The show opened up conversations between young people from the area, Bradford Council, Bradford Youth Service and West Yorkshire Police about the broader challenges of growing up in the city and encouraged those in professional roles to reflect on their treatment of young people.

## Site

Windhill Community Centre – a lively hub on the Windhill Estate where a brilliant team supports the community with a foodbank, cafe, advice hub and youth provision.

## Process

We hosted a three-day casting workshop drop-in at Windhill Community Centre and nobody came along. We continued visiting the youth centres around the area, meeting and talking to people. The sessions were often chaotic and it was difficult to speak to any of the young people when things were kicking off around us. In the end, via different routes and a lot of perseverance, we cast four young people with a range of experiences to bring to the show.

In the early sessions, we didn't do any drama at all, just an exercise where we'd print out questions about off-road vehicles, young people, friendship, relationships with services and the areas the cast lived in. We wrote the script from hours of questions and answers. We created original music, devised physical theatre sequences and went on filming adventures to iconic Bradford locations. We also brought in Kemmi Gill, a youth worker and young rapper, to perform and facilitate with us. An incredible performer in her own right, she helped to bridge the gap between the arts world and the world of the cast.

## Who

Performers: Kash, Rhys, James, Libby and Kemmi Gill
Directors: Saoirse Teale and Mariyah Kayat
Set and video design: Michelle Wren
Lighting design: Andy Purves
Sound design: Elliot Mann
Production manager: Tom Robbins
Stage manager: Kayleigh Chapman
Assistant director: David Bolitho

Funded by Bradford Community Safety Fund, Bradford Youth Service and Bradford Council.

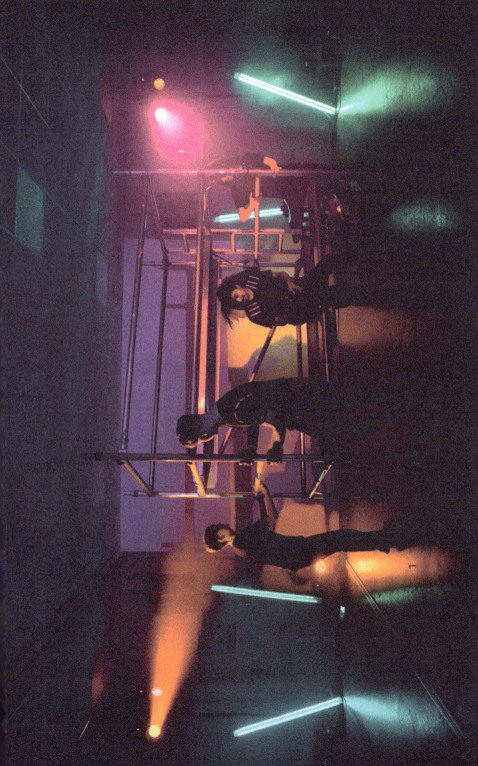

31 *Off Road*, Bradford, 2023. Credit: Daniel Johnson Gray

32 *Off Road*, Bradford, 2023. Credit: Daniel Johnson Gray

# FAST, FAST, SLOW (2023)

*Fast, Fast, Slow* invited its audiences to look at consumerism and waste through the lens of fast fashion. Staged on a catwalk of clothing bales with performers and collaborators from Blackburn and Burnley (UK), and Accra (Ghana).

## Seed

The British Textile Biennial were interested in exploring the relationship between first-, second- and third-generation migrants in Lancashire and the fashion industry. We were interested in this too, but as we started researching, we saw how the global networks of the fashion industry were now extending into Ghana, the world's biggest importer of second-hand clothing – a sector that has dramatically increased with the rise of fast fashion and throwaway clothes. The show became about capitalism and waste, and what we can learn from how Ghanaian market traders, campaigners and artists are responding.

## Context

*Fast, Fast, Slow* was about the fast pace and throwaway style that we live by in the Global North. During an R&D trip to Ghana we learned how much care is taken with thousands of bad-quality, broken garments arriving in massive clothing bales. We saw aisles and aisles of menders in the market who were upcycling, fixing, transforming garments that had been bought, worn once and thrown away.

## Site

The former Blackburn Cotton Exchange, built in 1865 and powered briefly by enslaved labour - a stark symbol of the destructive networks that the global textile industry has long been complicit with.

## Process

Our cast was made up of people with an interest in fashion from Blackburn and Burnley who held a real mix of attitudes. Saba had a thousand skirts, hundreds of items she'd only worn once; Carl bought quality clothes to last; Aneesah now restyles existing items having battled a clothes addiction; Ume Habiba and Eloise faced body dysmorphia; Chloe designed fantastical outfits that allow her to transcend reality. We honoured every person and ensured the show never judged them or their approach to fashion. Catwalk collections exploring themes such as 'Worn it once' and 'Clothes are my worst enemy' were brought to life by a cast of local performers aged 7 to 75 years old.

The Revival, a community-led organisation in Accra working with upcycled waste (therevival.earth) came on board as collaborators. During our trip to Ghana, we filmed immense clothes mountains with a local film crew and the Revival founders Kwamena and Yayra in their studio, talking directly through the camera to our UK audience. The film played throughout the show, gradually zooming out to reveal the mountains of fashion waste at full scale. At the end of the show, Kwamena 'steps through' the screen to appear in person on stage, saying the line, 'Imagine if we could see'. The film zooms out in slow motion – watching the images of the clothes mountains, we see they are located next to hundreds of houses and a river that flows into the sea. We zoom out from a small part of the picture to see the staggering, overwhelming reality of consumerism and waste and the connections between here and there.

## Who

Collaborators and performers: Saba Iftikhar, Carl Walker, Ume Habiba, Eloise Crossley, Aneesah Rashid, Chloe Northlight; The Revival – Kwamena Boison and Yayra Agbofa

Models and performers: Aminah Iftikhar, Safaa-Noor Ithikhar, Muskaan Khan, Tabinda Khauas, Nadia Iman Nazir, Stephen

O'Hagan, Falak Raja, Qaraman Mohammed Saidzada, Caelan Salmon, Kelly Semtungo, Lucy Eleanor Williams, Patricia Ann Willo Williams
Director: Evie Manning
Choreographer: May McQuade
Designer: Sascha Gilmour
Dramaturg: Sarah Thom
Film by Director Banini and crew (Producer: Ibrahim Adu; Sound: Fortunate Ayieb; Camera assistant: Benjamin Adjei; Drone: Kwame Isaac Ayinsu; Runner: King Faisal)
Composer and video design: Wojciech Rusin
Lighting design: Andy Purves

**33** *Fast, Fast, Slow*, Blackburn, 2023. Credit: Jack Bolton

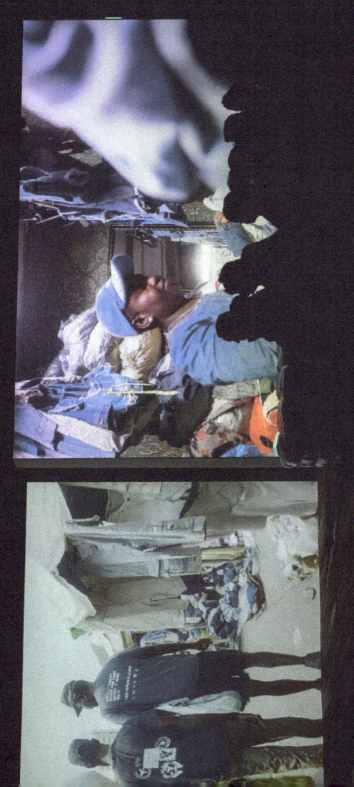

34 *Fast, Fast, Slow*, Blackburn, 2023. Credit: Jack Bolton

# OFF THE CURRICULUM (2023)

An immersive installation exploring subjects not taught in school through art forms not taught in school. Children and young people selected collisions of subjects and arts forms and figured out how they could work, designing a room based on their imagined pairing. A total of 16 rooms were transformed to explore: Capitalism + Graffiti, Jewellery + Time Travel, Greater Zimbabwe + Projection, Pottery + Self-Care, Deep Ocean + Puppetry, Kurdish Culture + Sculpture, Nature + Drawing, Natural Disasters + Clay, Climate Change + Den Building, Phones + Poetry, Arms Trade + Electronics, Origami + LGBTQI Rights, Gravity + Collage, Video Games + Fashion, Robots + Plants. There was also a room transformed into a new parliament, with debates led by the young people throughout the event.

## Seed

Evie's son, Remy, was at primary school and after a whole term in Year 3 (when he was eight years old) the only bit of 'art' in his artbook was a drawing of a rectangular picture frame. The walls of his classroom just had maths and English work pinned up. No art. It was depressing.

## Context

Arts and drama are actively being cut from state schools while being fostered in private schools. What does this do to the next generation of artists? In this context of art being valued for some and completely stripped away for working class kids, Off the Curriculum was a political statement about reclaiming the right of expression, play and curiosity.

## Site

Common Space, our Bradford base – a former youth opportunity centre that was due to be demolished.

## Process

- Brainstorm all the subjects you don't get taught at school and write them on separate pieces of paper.
- Then brainstorm all the art forms you don't get taught at school and write them on separate pieces of paper.
- Pair up a subject you don't get taught at school with an art form.
- Design a room based on this pairing.
- Work with a designer to draw up design sketches of your room.
- Give the designs to professional set builders and artists to bring to life.
- Design and facilitate a learning experience in your space.

We delivered this process with groups of young people and worked with eight set builders and artists who took the designs and made them happen, paying close attention to the designs so as to realise the vision of each kid. We created a wild three-day immersive learning festival. Each space was facilitated by the young person who designed it and there was a debate and a DJ set every half hour. Young people from All Star, the music studio who share Common Space with us, composed music based on *Off the Curriculum* subjects for the DJ set. We built 'New Parliament', a debating space where young people discussed subjects they chose, including:

- Does school take away individuality?
- Are working class and state school students disadvantaged?
- Should teachers go on strike?
- Exams shouldn't exist.
- Creative subjects are important academic subjects.
- Lunch breaks should be longer.
- Should uniform be mandatory?
- Is the education system racist?

# Who

Designed by: Musa, Remy, Scout, Coran, Zunaira, Zohaad, Reuben, Remi, Abigail, Jeremiah, Prue, Piper, Lily, Shifa, Rayyan, Scarlett, Abdul, Delia, Austin, Darcy, Aneesha, Nimrah, Habia, Humna, Noor, Amina, Aisha, Darisha, Sehrish, Zara, Laiba, Zaima, Rumaanah, Aishah, Anam, Saria, Safah, Eliyana, Aisha, Khadeejah, Macey, Savera, Jess, James, Noor, Axel, Becca, Fatima, Amina, Junaid, Khadija, Ameeliah, Safa, Lubabah, Aisha, Fareeha, Tori, Iman, Zeesth, Aaliya and Aaminah.

Built and brought to life by: Matt Sykes Hooban, Michelle Wren, Kazem Ashourzadeh, Cathy Cross, Hannah Sibai, Warda Abbasi, Naomi Parker, Robbie Thomson, Jamie Greir, Mariam Rashid, Sai Murray, Andy Purves, Hew Ma, Eleanor Barrett, Aamta-Tul Waheed, Trik 09, HIVE Bradford and All Star Entertainment.

## We wanted to think about Great Zimbabwe
*Off the Curriculum* collaborator, aged 12, Great Zimbabwe + Projection

We combined it with projection so we can really capture the ancient history that this room has. We wanted to think about Great Zimbabwe because at history at school it's a very short subject anyway – it's not really treated very well. But anyway, within the subjects you only get taught about the British and we never get taught about people who the British wronged. So this isn't just celebrating the culture of Great Zimbabwe, it's celebrating the culture of all the other civilisations that have been lost in the British Empire.

35 *Off the Curriculum*, Bradford, 2023. Credit: Karol Wyszynski

# WE NO LONGER TALK (2023)

*We No Longer Talk* was a 12-month creative and process-led project that explored different relationships with the Welsh language in working class communities in East Cardiff (South Wales) and Bethesda (North Wales).

## Seed

Rhiannon grew up in Cardiff in South Wales, not feeling particularly proud of where she came from. Her school didn't have the capacity to teach kids well and she didn't take Welsh lessons seriously. If she had been taught the history of Welsh culture, the activism behind the language, she might have fought more for it. Rhiannon met Ffion in Cardiff. Ffion was from a first-language Welsh-speaking working class family in North Wales. They created the concept of *We No Longer Talk* together – sharing contrasting experiences of class, place and Welsh language.

## Context

In Cardiff, the Welsh language has a middle class characteristic, with Welsh medium schools, Welsh learners and Welsh speakers far more prevalent in affluent parts of the city. In North Wales, the situation is the opposite – working class areas tend to be first-language Welsh, with Welsh spoken as part of everyday life. As the Senedd push for a million Welsh speakers by 2050, *We No Longer Talk* connected communities from East Cardiff (in the south) and Bethesda (in the north) for an honest conversation about the Welsh language.

## Site

This project originated in East Cardiff and travelled to sites across Wales, including Merthyr Tydfil, Tredegar, the Llŷn Peninsula, Y Bala, Capel Celyn, Caernarfon and Bethesda.

## Process

We had conversations with artists and activists from working class areas of Cardiff and across Wales about our relationship with the Welsh language and the history of Wales. We led workshops, read books and established Clwb Llyfrau Cymraeg in Cardiff, a weekly Welsh book club. Working with film maker Gavin Porter, we made a film poem, taking three artists from Cardiff who don't speak Welsh to collaborate with three Welsh-speaking artists from Bethesda.

## Who

Concept and direction: Rhiannon White and Ffion Wyn Morris
Film: Gavin Porter
Composition: Gwen Siôn
Film devised, written and performed by Ali Goolyad, Bedwyr Williams, Jude Thoburn-Price, Liws, Rhys Trimble and Thaer Al-Shayei

36 *We No Longer Talk*, Bethesda, 2024. Credit: Gavin Porter

# WORKS-INITIATIVES

It isn't all about the shows! We've always been about having a wider purpose in our home cities. So, we're closing the book with descriptions of four of our long-running initiatives in Bradford and Cardiff. The people involved in each of these initiatives have played a crucial role in keeping us inspired, connected and relevant, generating new energy and purpose, keeping our feet on the ground and keeping us going. We're grateful and pleased to be able to include some of their voices in this book.

# SPEAKERS CORNER

Mariyah Kayat

## What is Speakers Corner Collective?

Speakers Corner is a social, creative and political space where young women come together to explore topics that are important to us. We've campaigned on body image, bridging generational gaps, drone strikes, mental health, war, violence against women, Islamophobia and many more issues.

Speakers Corner is about sisterhood. You get to meet, make friends and work with people that you wouldn't meet anywhere else. There is work to do, and it's with people who care about you, want the best for you and support you. It's a safe space, where you can be open. There's no judgement.

The social, political and creative are all meshed together. There are politics in everything we do. Whether it's an exhibition, or designing a flyer, or making a comic, there's always some form of creativity. It's social in that we are young women coming together, every Wednesday. There's a lot of activity, but Speakers Corner can also be a space to just hang out.

We're youth led. We decide. We manage the budget. We do the social media. It's very much our thing. Common/Wealth supports us and we feed into lots of Common/Wealth shows, projects and how the company runs but from the beginning it was important for Speakers Corner to have its own identity.

## How we started

Speakers Corner started with a campaign called *I Am Perfect as Me*, which was about what makes us who we are and saying that those things make us perfect, flaws and all. Young people feeling confident in themselves and having that confidence in their bodies. Afterwards we started meeting in an empty shop in Bradford. It was us, every day after school, coming to town on the bus. We'd get a drink, get some food, come to Speakers Corner.

## Some of our campaigns

*Justice in Kashmir Is Justice Here.* It was the 30-year anniversary of mass violence and rape against women in the village of Kunan Poshpora in Kashmir. The military law there meant that no one could speak about it. Even when people had collected evidence and tried to take it to court, nobody got punished. We're privileged in where we live in that we can speak out. One of us, aged 15 years and in her first ever campaign, wrote a poem, and we made a film with her speaking the poem as the voiceover. We made a comic strip and pasted it onto billboards all around Bradford. We got a lot of press coverage.

*Swim with Speakers.* You go swimming when you're in primary school but you don't become a confident swimmer. A lot of people only feel comfortable in women-only sessions, but those sessions are very few. We applied to Sport England for funding to run women-only sessions with a female instructor. We paid for transport, charged £1 a session and taught nearly 100 women how to swim. People had different abilities – some were super confident just swimming back and forth, others terrified of being in water. There were young women, older women, women who didn't speak a lot of English. Everyone was just in the water, learning how to swim and being together.

*Take a Breath* focused on health and well-being. We applied for a pot of money and ran events through the summer. We wanted to focus on mental health but provide an alternative to the approach you always get, which isn't always helpful. We were aware that some young people were struggling to get out and finding it hard to be in groups after COVID. We did candle decorating, pottery making, cycling, netball and strawberry picking. We paid for travel and took away that barrier of cost. At the end we did 'know your rights', with self-defence classes and rights training. We looked at how to keep yourself safe, how to keep other people safe and what to do if someone challenges you in public.

## It's called Speakers Corner *Collective*

There's power in being a collective. Everyone has a voice and has something to say. It goes from being my idea to this big thing and you forget who started it. Someone will say something, and you're like, yes, that annoys me too. You're bonded over it and there's that fire. As a group, we've made this work.

## What's next for Speakers Corner?

I joined Speakers Corner in 2017, aged 16 years. I've been part of so many different campaigns. I became a Common/Wealth apprentice in 2019 and that became a paid position – I'm now Speakers Corner Producer. We want to create a new kind of mental health practice, where we do our creative campaign work alongside professional mental health support. Speakers Corner has always had a big South Asian demographic. A lot of young people of colour struggle with mental health and with accessing services. As a young person of colour myself, I understand the barriers. It's not really talked about – you're struggling and going through stuff, but who do you go to for support? Will they understand? There are massive waiting lists and many young people have had more than one bad experience with services and so there is distrust. To have those services in an already established safe space feels like a no brainer to me.

37 Speakers Corner, Bradford. Credit: Karol Wyszynski

# THE SOUNDING BOARD

Of course, they look for a shit hole, get the money and then fuck off. Basically, it is what has been happening for so many years. But we come along, and we are different, and people can see that: 'Oh, wow, you're still here.' We do the mural, the exhibition, the Posh Club, the shows, and their mums and dads, and nanas and bampis are going there and having a good time. And the ripples from what you have been doing over a couple of years are now extending out, filling up and swelling. That can be taken forward with feeling and hopefulness. I have been doing community work for 40-odd years here, and the hopefulness was extinguished when they knocked all the community centres down and when they knocked down the shops. Everything was closed. So it was like, 'Well, you lot, you can just fuck off and die because we're not interested in the lower classes'.

Jude, Sounding Board

Common/Wealth started renting an office in Llanrumney in East Cardiff in 2020, building a Welsh home for the company in the heart of a council estate. Our mission was to explore what it might mean for an arts organisation to work in, from and with its working class community to reimagine the role of theatre and activism at neighbourhood level. What does it mean to be artists in residence over the long term and to collaborate closely with our neighbours? Where can we stage our work? How do we build audiences and artists, and respond directly to emerging needs? Who do we need to work with? How do we build a movement?

## The Sounding Board

The Sounding Board is a group of working class people from across South Wales who are interested in art and social change and creating opportunities for people and places to thrive.

When we established a base in East Cardiff, we knew we couldn't create a home by ourselves; we wanted and needed to collaborate directly with the community to build something that made sense to the place we were making roots in. We recruited 12 people who were passionate about our mission: residents, artists, mums, musicians, youth workers, community leaders and teachers – people who were hungry for change and cared deeply about creating an artistic offer for working class people.

This is not a steering group or a board. It is more than that. This is a movement of people meeting to imagine something different, active, activist, pushing for change. We are each other's arms and legs and our eyes and ears. It is a symbiotic relationship. We support each other to do things and, most importantly, to dream.

When you come from a place that has been demonised, ground down and has had limited access to opportunities, resources and education, the starting point is often negative: 'Nothing happens here, no one gives a shit, why would they come?' Our mission was to flip the switch.

We knew we needed a crew who believed in the dream as much as we did, a support network, drivers who could keep us pushing, keep us imagining and being ambitious. Holding true alongside the people who live and breathe a place helps us focus and keep moving forward.

Systems can seem designed to extinguish hope and possibility. Our mission is to build on hope through imagination and, most importantly, making art. With our experts, the Sounding Board, we make decisions about things that will happen in the neighbourhood, aiming to bring back some hope and to share a sense of possibility.

Every member of our Sounding Board brings a different perspective. It's a long game; cumulative knowledge and skill are built over time. We watch the ripples, opportunities, and people grow and develop into something beyond Common/Wealth.

# The Sounding Board: in conversation
Poppy Horwood, Callum Lloyd, David Melkevik, Nel Philip, Jude Thoburn-Price, Stephanie Rees

## *A whole learning journey*

We've had this whole learning journey, and now everyone's knowledge and skills are on the table, ready to be used. All our brains coming together to collaborate generates possibility and opportunity. It's been amazing to encounter artists and art-making first hand. We've done writing, theatre-making, storytelling, set-building, visual arts, dance and acting workshops. All the artists were really generous. Every artist who has come here has given us a bit more information about what we want as a company. We've worked with talented, incredible artists – people we never thought would come here.

## *Everyone is an artist*

Exposure to the work of so many artists has shown that there are different ways of telling a story and making theatre. Each year, we run a free workshop programme called 'Everyone is an Artist'. It's about inviting exceptional artists to our community. We want a range of offers so every person gets a chance to experience being creative somehow. We help programme 'Everyone is an Artist' – we think about what would work, how it could be delivered, where and for whom. These experiences have made us better at decision-making.

We ran a Radical Grime School in partnership with the youth service (where one of us works) and listened to how and why the artists were into grime and what their music meant to them. Our young people have stories to tell, and that's how they tell them. We created a music performance with them and invited their parents. At one point we had 40-plus kids in the room.

Some of us don't come from theatre backgrounds. For us, theatre meant being in dark rooms, singing and dancing. That's all great, but it doesn't engage people from this area and isn't relevant to them. But showing them a performance in the neighbourhood, in a house or a community centre is exciting for them.

## Theatre and neighbourhood: the journey matters

It is about the journey. The journey matters. The journey that people go on is as important, if not more important, than the show itself. The more enabled and encouraged, the better the end product is anyway. Common/Wealth believes in process and production in equal measure, paying attention to both and supporting the work to evolve and keep moving.

We're on a journey to build on how Common/Wealth exists in our neighbourhood and how we also exist. What we need, what others need, how we can create and support each other for the future. It's all developing and growing in tandem. It's about social change too: what can we do to shift perspective, tell a different story about working class people, bring people together and create more working class artists.

We make space for politics. In our theatre work we've connected with women in the West Bank and Gaza, talked about climate justice through a working class lens, and talked about austerity and its effect on our community. We have a book club, inspired by the miners and their reading rooms. Each week we meet to read together, whether it's about police injustice, Palestine or the history of Welsh activism. From that, we've started Clwb Llyfrau Cymraeg, our Welsh-language book club, where we read in Welsh no matter what our level of language ability is.

## Rediscovering our place

Not much happens arts-wise in East Cardiff, so it's exciting to have something happening here on the doorstep. There's a real sense of adventure about being part of the Sounding Board. We go for walks and notice the landscapes and their history and the impact that certain things have had. Imagine where things could be performed; this landscape is our stage, and anything could happen here.

We hear a lot that there's no sense of community. Then you do a show locally and you see community. You bring them all together and they have the most amazing time. All these people were already there.

When you are in a place that is so used to being overlooked, when something comes here – no matter how much good it's trying to do – there is distrust. It takes a long time to build trust. There is a lack of willing engagement before people go, 'Oh, you're not going anywhere. You're still here.' We have been able to develop a sustained partnership with Duckie's Posh Club which – at the time of writing – sees us offering a regular swanky afternoon tea with performance acts to people aged over 60 in the community. The success of Posh Club filters down to the younger generations, because the people who come tell their children and grandchildren about it. Next time something comes up, they'll be saying, 'That's what my nan goes to. I'm going to go and have a look.'

For far too long, artists have dropped in, made a piece of work, taken the funding, drawn from the community and gone off to exploit somebody else. The things we've commissioned are drops of water in a pond. They make a ripple. We watch to see where the ripples go and what they connect to. Those things come back into our sphere and we take what is there and work with it. We give it a go. See what works well. What was shit. 'Okay, that was shit, we won't do that again', but the good things, we take them forward. We keep doing that and, each time, you get a bigger and better ripple.

## Our ripples so far

There have been many ripples, things we are proud of and that are growing, shifting and developing in so many ways. We see them as starting points, the inspiration – the movement we love and care about.

For Stephie, being part of the Sounding Board provided the impetus to set up a local arts organisation Breakthrough Theatre Arts, a leading provision for kids to attend, make and showcase their work. Sharing co-creation and making shows is at the heart of the project as it connects with working class kids across South Wales.

Jude was cast in Payday Party, which went from being staged in an East Cardiff Conservative Club to sell-out audiences and then on to the Edinburgh Fringe as part of the Welsh Showcase.

For Poppy, being part of the Sounding Board informed the creation of a disabled-led theatre company that she and her friends have set up.

Our Sounding Board members have won awards, been part of incredible projects like Posh Club, performed at our sharing of the Gaza Monologues, spoken at conferences in London on co-creation and been part of many projects that have moved from the local to the global, and that's the important bit. Although the Sounding Board is based in East Cardiff, we look outwards – for inspiration, for work, for ideas and perspectives that can be part of a global conversation and movement.

> It's a sense of belonging to the land, place, time and people. And they know that it's like planting seeds. And they know that by caring for the seed, even if it's put on a shit piece of earth, they can nurture it to be the best it can be. You're building a beautiful garden, and we get to visit it. You're also giving us the skills of working in the garden growing. Because we're doing that, we become even more invested in these things succeeding.
> 
> Jude, Sounding Board

38 Sounding Board, Cardiff, 2020. Credit: Camilla Brueton

# YOUTH THEATRE LAB

Saoirse Teale

## What is Youth Theatre Lab?

Youth Theatre Lab is a creative and social space for young people aged from 11 to 18. It's one of Common/Wealth's strands of work by, with and for young working class people in Bradford, alongside Speakers Corner. Youth Theatre Lab meets weekly on a Friday evening, and we make new performance work drawing on young people's experiences.

## How we work

When we set up the youth theatre, we wanted to do it differently from the youth theatres I'd worked in previously. To offer a creative space for all young people in Bradford, we needed a youth theatre that didn't cost money to attend. We also didn't want it to be solely focused on theatre, because theatre can feel inaccessible to a lot of people. We made our youth theatre interdisciplinary (all art forms welcome), social and food-orientated. It's not just theatre – it's music, dance, movement, live art, comedy, drag, whatever the young people want it to be. That's the first hour each Friday night. And in the last half hour we order pizza, put the sound system on, have a dance, have a sing, gossip, make reels, whatever the young people want to do.

## How we started

We sent the word out to Bradford Youth Service, the Looked After Children team, schools and via social media. Nowadays we do workshops in schools, we speak at youth events and take the kids to speak as well – a lot of people know we're here. Word travels with the young people who come. They're the best advertisers.

## How to build and grow

In the early days, it was really bloody awkward. In the first session, nobody would say their name out loud. They wouldn't play games. They would just look at us like they wanted to die. And we realised, nobody in the room had ever been to a theatre to see shows, and they'd never been to a group outside of school. They had no reference point for what we were trying to do. They didn't really know what they were signing up for. It took really slow, tender, caring work. Starting from scratch. No 'acting', just lots of chatting and gentle live art exercises. This went on for months. We did it every Friday. We had 12 people in that first week, and three years later, 9 of them are still with us as well as about 10 more.

We've had different chapters. In the first chapter, the kids performed their own piece, an exploration of street harassment, at Leeds Playhouse. They arrived at one session really angry about getting cat-called in town. We were like, 'you guys all have stuff to say'. Common/Wealth works in that way – you make work about real stuff you have experienced. Your voice is heard. We see and hear you – you're angry, we're angry, let's make work about it. You can say what you want to say, you can swear – it doesn't have to be pretty.

They'd never seen theatre performed before, and they got to perform at Leeds Playhouse. After that, they clicked. 'Ah, this is what it is!' We were different from the other groups there. The kids were performing their own experiences. The group was diverse, and there was embedded youth work going on.

In the next chapter, they understood the art form more and created more devised work. We made a new piece, *One Way System*, as part of *Off the Curriculum*, exploring their different experiences of the school system. Some of the young people in our group don't go to school – some are home educated and some just hate school. Then we made *The Games They Play*, a piece exploring young people's perspectives on UK and international politics, told through the playing of board and party games.

In our current chapter, Youth Theatre Lab members are taking on more of a leadership role, expanding the scale and form of projects they work on. This involves building up their directing skills, devising a new, exciting piece of site-specific theatre with a collective of young people from Germany.

As the youth element of Common/Wealth has grown, we wanted an annual moment to celebrate our young people and so we developed the 29% Festival (29% of Bradford's population is under 19, making it the youngest city in Europe). It's a multi-art weekender featuring young artists, designed and delivered by young people, who also support with fundraising, outreach, marketing and programming ideas, as well as performing, exhibiting and facilitating their own work.

## Youth Theatre Lab reflections

I think young people are underestimated in the world, especially when it comes to addressing political issues. We're always told we're not old enough to understand the world but we have a lot of opinions and beliefs. Common/Wealth let us portray that out to the world. I might be 17 but I understand that this is happening. When it comes to accessibility, don't shame anyone. As someone who's physically disabled and sometimes just has to take a break, we are never like, 'Oh, its theatre, you have to have a high stamina'. It's a safe space in that sense as well. A lot of people are worried about theatre being very competitive and very driven. But here there's a lot more leniency and comfort in the way we work.

Hania

It was very much – what have you got to say? What are your ideas? It wasn't really them telling us what to do. As a young person, stuff like the news, you don't take it seriously. Especially now, when the whole world's going a bit mad. Youth Theatre Lab makes you think about it and it also gives a way to express your views and your frustrations in a creative way.

Jess

Youth Lab is a space where you're learning, and educating yourself, about politics, about the world. You get a creative outlet for how to actually formulate your opinions and express yourself. You have a voice as a young person. It's a way to actually get people involved in politics and to start thinking about bigger issues, and to encourage people to educate themselves on it. There are different talents that people bring, and different views. You don't have to have done acting or drama before. It's more about whether you have something you want to say. You learn all these skills, you make friendships, you make memories. It doesn't have to be anything to do with political activity. It could just be for yourself, developing skills, life skills, meeting people.

Noor

39 Youth Theatre Lab, Bradford, 2024. Credit: Pishdaad Modaressi

# PERFORMANCE COLLECTIVE

The Performance Collective is a group of nine young creatives who participated in a year-long paid training programme to develop skills as performance makers and facilitators. Following the year-long programme, the Performance Collective has extended to encompass other young people under 35 years old who meet monthly.

The aim is to galvanise the next generation of working class artists. To provide a 360-degree set of skills, a network of contacts, and opportunities to develop creative work and learn skills. So many people have a creative soul and it's difficult to know how to channel this, and so the Performance Collective is about bringing young creatives together to find power in the collective, building confidence and ambition together – valuing the common wealth.

The collective have a mixture of creative interests and experiences, spanning visual and live arts, music, performance, DJing, dance, writing and spoken word.

## The Performance Collective: in conversation

**Samara:** If we're going to be honest about how the creative scene works, there aren't many opportunities out there for people. I came to Bradford as a care leaver and I've spent 10 years in limbo, just trying to get my foot in, struggling financially, trying to make sure I had some stability. Here I've learned to be a bit more open and not hold on so tightly to a creative process, and not to completely delete things when it goes wrong. It's helping me to reshape how I write, how I perform and to develop my style. It's also informing how I do community work. I'm a committee member of Checkpoint, a Caribbean community association in Bradford. Being part of the Performance Collective is helping me think through how to develop more of a creative community there. Before this opportunity, I didn't think about being a freelance creative, but since coming here, I've started to actually understand what that means and to see how to make it work. My friends don't think I can be a successful creative: 'You don't come from a rich family, you don't have this and that.' But here, I can see that there are a lot of things I can do with what I've already done.

**Nabeel:** I came into this as a blank canvas. I didn't know what to expect. If you told me at the start that I'd feel comfortable dancing and performing I would have said you're out of your mind. It's helped me feel more at ease doing things outside my comfort zone. I'd say my interests are in film and TV, and I've met people here who are into similar stuff. I imagine myself behind the camera, but the performance side of things has improved my confidence. I've grown a lot in that respect. I realised the only way I could do it is if I threw myself into it. The collaborative spirit here is also important. There's no ownership of ideas. We come up with ideas together and most of the time it morphs into something better. Having a lot of the guests and people from the industry, getting their perspectives and learning their techniques has been really fun.

**Yasmin:** When this opportunity presented itself, I was like, what is this? The offer was really unique. I've always loved live art and theatre. It was a genuine dream of mine to perform and be a part of a theatre community. In my early years, this wasn't attainable due to financial reasons. I am so grateful to be among a like-minded creative community, where we are encouraged and share a powerful mission to campaign for sociopolitical change. We are learning so much. It feels collective. Sometimes that can be a buzzword. Is it really collective? Are we all shining? We all arrived here at Common/Wealth and were encouraged to express our own understanding of the world and our stories, as they make us who we are. But we also come together collectively and share an energy that enables us to put forward our ideas and thoughts. It's so refreshing. Overall, this is a huge engine of possibilities. It's sustainable in the way of thinking that the company has, and that now we all have, which is about resourcefulness.

**Kenzie:** For me, it's the multidisciplinary space that we've got. In Bradford, you've got your artists over here, your DJs over there, your musicians over there, your poets over here. Here everyone can come together and be in one space. We're from different backgrounds, and we've managed to come together. Being in a mixed group like this – it is where better ideas come from, because everyone sees things from a different perspective. Everyone's skills get utilised. It is fully collaborative. One of us comes up with an idea, we'll build on it and it becomes a group idea that is 10 times better than where it started. Since I've been here, I've become more independent in what I'm doing. This time last year, I wouldn't have shared my music with anyone. I would have kept it all private. Now I actually need to share it. I need all opinions on it. I've become more comfortable doing things for myself and putting myself more out there.

**Mahshid:** It has offered a very big boost of confidence for me. We learned a big variety of skills that let me call myself a performer and live performance maker. We create a lot of things. After taking part in these experiences, I see myself as a person who comes up with ideas and who makes things, more than just performs things. Being with these amazing people, I have learned how to be in a team and how we can look after each other without competing. Next time I join a group, I will have very high expectations.

**Mustafa:** When I saw the advertisement, I wasn't sure whether to go for it. I don't believe in politics. I believe that politicians just vote for their pocket, not for the interests of the people. But I thought, let's try it. My experience before was to be on stage, performing material that is already ready. You rehearse and you present the show. But here, we plan something from zero. And there is nothing 100% certain. We make something from the beginning to the end, whereas before I was part of things from the middle point to the end. I really enjoy it. Also getting to know everyone and experience their creativity. I learn something from everybody and everybody's good at something. I'm also taking something away about support. Support means support as a group. Sometimes to support the group is to step in and take the bullet for the group. And sometimes support means stepping out, and making a decision that, if I step in, it may be chaos. You step out to keep the balance.

**Sarah:** I started training in screen acting. A lot of the time, when performing, you are just told what to do. You are a character and this is what you do. Here, it's unlearning all that to just be in front of an audience. Us actors like to heighten ourselves when we are in front of an audience and it's been really interesting to learn how to peel that back, be vulnerable in a space and have really open and honest conversations. And to learn how to have a collective mindset. We think about theatre, traditionally speaking, as entertainment. You go along for a distraction, which is great, but it's a limited understanding of theatre. Coming here, you learn that it can be so much more than that. I'm going forward knowing how the arts can be an accessible and engaging way for people to learn about politics, and to learn about what's going on in the world. Theatre and the arts are not just for entertainment – they can be used for so much more.

**Jojo:** I've been in this country for eight months and I don't know much about the theatre culture here. This has been an eye-opener for me. I have a theatre background – I studied theatre at university for four years. I've been in the theatre space for quite a while. But coming here you get involved with people learning and you are doing research and development stuff. Back home in Nigeria, you're just getting told what to do. You get given a role in a play, you learn your lines, develop your character and perform. Here, you're building everything from scratch. And you are involved in the creation from the beginning. You're invested in the process. You're working with people in a collective way. Everybody is responsible for the other person in terms of how you feel, how you work and all of that. It's a different process, a more engaging process, and all of that makes you feel more confident and free to express and explore.

**Noor:** The planning of performance has been interesting, rather than performing itself. It has been useful exploring different aspects such as the emotional score or using stage space to our advantage. It is nice having this control to evoke a certain emotion, stimulate thinking and send out a message. It has also been interesting to learn and see these skills in action. Our first show, In Common, was extremely helpful in putting things into perspective, allowing reflection that led to improvements. But this whole process of planning has enabled me to appreciate theatre more – the thought that goes behind it all. I am in awe of how impactful it can be. I have found myself feeling more creative and confident, as well as willing to challenge myself, whether that be writing or movement. I particularly enjoy the planning conversations, where I have not just learned more about the people I work with, but also feel more aware of myself.

## Reflecting on the Performance Collective – Evie

Setting up the Performance Collective, writing this book, the way we go about making our shows with people new to performance – it's always been about opening a door for people to step into being artists. We're aware of how opportunities to become artists are fewer and fewer for working class people. In England, art, drama and music have been cut back in state-funded education. University fees have tripled and lack of investment in the arts across the UK continues to create financial insecurity and unstable careers for artists. The times we live in can make it feel more difficult to find, meet up and connect with each other, and these difficulties can feel even more challenging for those of us living outside of better resourced, richer areas. But still kids dance on garden walls, paint, put on plays with their mates. Creativity is innate, and it's everywhere. It's important. And we can't lock it up. It's necessary to dream, to play, to disrupt, to gather. The Performance Collective was about creating an outlet for that. It's so important to find your people, at your community centre, at a dance class, with some mates in your living room. And then to be ambitious within that, playing, watching, sharing work and dreaming things up together.

40 Performance Collective, Bradford, 2024. Credit: Pishdaad Modaressi

# AFTERWORD

Thank you for reading this book. Now go and do it yourself.

# INDEX

29% Festival 196, 323

Ahmed, Casper 264, 265-8
Ahmed, Zia 195
Altowai, Shatha 252-9
Anah Project 251
arms trade 23, 26, 52, 136, 251, 253, 258, 295
arts council 7, 11, 16, 17, 36, 165, 166, 181, 194, 195
Ashtar Theatre 26
audience, audiences xi, 24, 28, 29, 30, 32, 33-5, 45, 49, 51, 66, 72-3, 76, 77, 99, 119, 123, 125-7, 135, 144-5, 146, 148, 151-2, 155, 163, 179-80, 182, 219, 242, 258, 259, 266, 267, 268, 330
austerity 15, 18, 49, 55, 192, 205, 316
see also bedroom tax

BBC 20, 217
bedroom tax 193
Bethesda 301-2
Bevan, Aneurin 13, 229
Black Lives Matter 193, 194
body 70-1, 78-80, 81-3, 88-9
Bradford 6, 9-11, 15-16, 20, 45, 51, 52, 54, 56, 123-4, 136, 159-60, 208, 215, 216-17, 217-18, 219, 243, 283, 323
  Bradford City Hall 54, 223
  Bradford Club 53, 54, 243
  Bradford Modified Car Club 244, 263
Brecht, Bertolt 29, 181, 201-2
Brexit 223, 230, 193, 194
Bristol 5, 14-15, 201
Brith Gof 29
British Textile Biennial 289
Brown, Gordon 192
budgeting 147, 161, 163, 165, 167-8, 307
Brueton, Camilla 155

campaign 18, 23-4, 31, 32, 54, 56, 101, 159, 161, 205, 223, 243, 307, 308-9
  see also Campaign Against the Arms Trade, JENGbA, Trade Justice Movement, Save Our Steel, unions, Women's Aid
Campaign Against the Arms Trade 23
capitalism xv, 1, 19, 23, 48-9, 53, 129, 231, 289 295
cardboard 25, 128-9, 130, 201
Cardiff 6, 12-13, 16, 45, 194, 273, 301-2
  East Cardiff 34, 50, 55-6, 150-1, 179, 194, 273-4, 276, 301, 313, 316, 318
  East Cardiff Conservative Club 318
  see also Llanrumney, St Mellons
Casson, Simon 179
  see also Duckie
casting 40, 73-4, 252, 284
Chapter Arts Centre 13
Chumbawamba 20
Circus 2 Palestine 14, 192
cleaning 40, 145, 146
co-creation 38-9, 318
colonial history 18-19, 23, 253
commissioning 165, 166, 173, 273, 317
common 5, 6-8, 9-14, 17, 21, 24, 26, 30-1, 50
commons 19
Common Space 15, 56-7, 194, 295-6
communication 41, 51, 109, 167
  see also conversation
composition 83, 276-8
  composing and sound design 139-143
Contact 217
conversation 1, 5, 17, 31, 33-5, 41, 46-7, 48, 68-9, 108, 123, 151, 155, 157, 166, 205-6, 218, 243, 258, 259, 263, 274, 283, 301-2

INDEX 337

Corbyn, Jeremy 193, 243
council house, housing 12, 16, 50
council estate 12, 13, 179, 216, 274, 313
creative industries 7
cultural democracy 39

dance 8, 54, 71, 78, 79, 82, 83, 94, 179, 181, 182, 321, 331
Dartington College of Arts 13–14
*The Deal Versus the People* 28, 54, 193, 222–5
Deller, Jeremy 144
devising 72–7, 94–6, 99–100, 123, 142
directing 17–18, 119–20
DIY Culture 5, 14, 131, 192
documenting 32, 173, 276–8
domestic violence 12–13, 50, 122, 205–6
dreaming 19, 23, 36, 45, 48, 56, 75, 120, 135, 182, 314, 331
Duckie 176, 179, 196, 317
  see also Casson, Simon
Dunican, Ali 164, 172

Edinburgh Festival 216, 318
Eley, Alexander 252–9
Emotion, emotional 1, 26, 30, 75, 139, 258
emotional score 72, 73, 99–100, 108, 109, 216, 330–1
evaluation 32, 77, 117–8
Evans, David 144
experimental performance 1, 5, 6, 13, 16, 27–8, 28–9, 45, 50, 94–6

*Fast, Fast, Slow* 95, 195, 228–91
fix+foxy 29
Forensic Architecture 29
Fragments Theatre 81
Freedom Programme 206
The Freedom Theatre 29, 259
friends 5, 14, 20–1, 36, 37, 39, 66, 101, 106, 129, 181
Fuel Productions 51, 265

funding 6, 7, 11, 15, 16, 25, 36, 56, 112, 131, 163, 164–71, 207, 317

games 12, 78, 91–2, 104, 160
gang see friends
Gates, Theaster 29
Gaza 14, 192, 193, 195, 215
  Gaza Monologues 26, 318
Ghana 289–90
  see also The Revival
ghosts 9, 47–50, 55, 73, 135, 142
Gill, Kemmi 284
Gob Squad 29
Goldsmiths University 9–10, 128
Gordon, Avery 47, 48–9

Hardie, Keir 229
hope, hopefulness xv, 23, 36, 313, 314

*I Have Met the Enemy (and the enemy is us)* 26, 52, 136, 194, 250–9, 265
impact 31–2, 150, 172–3, 253, 266
interviews 34, 46, 73, 90, 100, 108–10, 111, 123, 124, 126, 206, 208, 216, 230
Invisible Circus 179, 201
Islam 264, 267
Islamophobia 51, 244, 263, 264, 266, 307

Jellicoe, Ann 144
Johnson, Boris 194
Joint Enterprise Not Guilty by Association (JENGbA) 23
Jones, Patrick 13

Kayat, Mariyah 159, 306
Khoury, Tania El 29

lighting 96, 111, 133–8
Llanrumney 250, 322, 369
Lung Theatre 29
local council 36, 56, 106, 146, 148
London 10, 16, 33, 131

Mahamdallie, Hassan 255
Mahmood, Seherish 217-19
Manning, Remy 10-11, 295
Marx, Karl 48
McGrath, John 16, 125
McQuade, May 155
May, Theresa 194
Moving Roots 194, 195

Nash, Ezra 155
National Theatre Wales 16, 125, 133, 144, 175, 193
neighbourhood 55-6, 112-13, 150-3, 313-14, 316
networks see friends
No Guts, No Heart, No Glory 29, 51-2, 88, 96, 123-4, 140-2, 193, 214-19
Northern Stage 251, 252

Occupy Movement 192
Off Road 129, 160-1, 195, 282-4
Off the Curriculum 28, 57, 195, 294-7, 322
optimism see hope
Our Glass House 11, 15, 50-1, 93, 100, 109-10, 122-4, 139, 159, 192, 193, 195, 204-9, 217
Owen, Gary 231, 234-8

Palestine 14, 17, 26, 52, 56, 82, 251, 316
partnership 16, 34, 41, 51, 54, 106, 118, 166, 167, 170, 172, 173-4, 206, 315, 317
Paul Hamlyn Foundation 194
Peaceophobia 51, 53, 95, 100, 101-2, 135-6, 194, 195, 244, 262-8, 283,
Perth, Australia 51, 216
play, playing 1, 8, 9, 28, 49, 71, 75, 78, 83, 104, 105, 113, 120, 134, 141, 160, 235, 331
political theatre xii, xv, 19, 26-8, 30, 121-4, 125-7, 259
Port Talbot xi, 48, 126-7, 143, 193, 194, 229, 231, 233, 234, 237
The Posh Club 176, 179, 195, 196, 313, 317

Pountney, Jon 276-8, 279
power xi, xv, 20, 26-7, 45, 47, 48-9, 53, 78, 91-2, 124, 125, 133, 137, 209, 224, 257, 273, 276, 309, 327
pregnancy 10-11, 192, 194
press 16, 33, 40-1, 175-8, 278, 308
Pritchard, Darren 195
producing 150-3, 154-8
protest 36, 56, 127, 215, 229, 233
    anti-protest legislation 195
Purves, Andy 133-8

queer 162, 181, 182
questions 30-1, 32, 54, 66, 69, 72, 99, 100, 104, 108-10, 112, 117-18, 123, 137, 206, 252, 257, 284

racism 6, 18, 136, 216, 267
Radical Acts 26, 53, 54, 84-5, 137, 194, 242-7, 263
rehearsing, rehearsal 18, 35, 38, 54, 86-7, 109, 111, 119-20, 142, 206, 215, 216, 218, 230, 255, 264, 267
research and development (R&D) 75, 108, 128, 140, 142, 154, 166, 216, 255, 264, 266
reviews 33
The Revival 23, 290
ripples see impact
Rogers, Catrin 176-8
Roy, Arundhati 48
Rusin, Wojciech 139-43

Save Our Steel xi, 193, 229, 232
Senedd Cymru 195, 274, 301
set design 28, 52, 57, 74, 128-32
site-specific performance 5, 6, 45-6, 50-1, 55-6, 77, 139, 144-9, 180
Slee, Jane 231-4
Starmer, Keir 196
socialism 13
Sopal, Balvinder 207-9
Sounding Board 152-3, 194, 275, 312-18

Speakers Corner 11, 26, 51, 56, 57, 159, 193, 194, 244, 263–4, 266, 267, 306–9
squatting 11, 15, 106, 128, 131–2, 201
St Mellons 12, 176, 179, 273–5, 276
Swaitat, Mo'min 252–9

tasks 83, 94–6, 104
Tata Steel 48, 229, 231, 232, 233
Teale, Saoirse 159, 320
Thatcher, Margaret 55
theatre buildings 1, 5, 25, 45, 46, 135, 154–5
theatre industry 7, 24, 25, 34
ticket prices 35, 53, 178, 234
Touretteshero 29
touring 6, 50–2, 172–4, 216
  touring site-specific performance 50–1
Trade Justice Movement 23, 54, 223
Transatlantic Trade Investment Partnership (TTIP) 54, 223
Trezise, Rachel xi, 125–7
Trump, Donald 194, 196

The Underdogs 12, 150
unions 21, 31, 125, 167, 230

verbatim 121, 206, 207–9, 235

war xv, 6, 14, 52, 250–2, 252–3, 254, 255, 258, 259

welfare benefits 5, 11, 49, 193
Welfare State International 29
Welsh language 301–2, 316
*We're Still Here* xi, 28, 48–9, 125–7, 135, 140, 142–3, 145, 193, 194, 228–38
Williams, Chantal 12, 33–4, 150–3
Williams, Raymond 6
Women's Aid 23
working class 5, 7, 17, 19, 24, 55, 111, 114, 179–80, 229, 274, 276–8, 301, 313–14
  working class artists 131, 132, 163, 295, 302, 316, 327, 331
  working class audiences 20, 28, 46, 179–82
Wren, Michelle 128–32
writing 86, 97–8, 121–4, 125–7, 244, 245

Yemen 52–3, 193, 251, 252, 252–3, 254, 256, 257–8
young people 9, 28, 45, 51–2, 56–7, 135, 157, 159–63, 283–4, 295–6, 307–9, 321–3
Youth Theatre Lab 57, 159–63, 162, 195, 320–4

Zia, Aisha 121–4

EU authorised representative for GPSR:
Easy Access System Europe, Mustamäe tee 50,
10621 Tallinn, Estonia
gpsr.requests@easproject.com

www.ingramcontent.com/pod-product-compliance
Lightning Source LLC
LaVergne TN
LVHW071203200925
821343LV00069B/876